100 vegetarian recipes

Did you like this book?

You can leave a review on its page

BILER RUPENSE

Copyright © 2023 Biler Rupense.
Paris.
All rights reserved.
Print on demand.
Legal deposit December 2023
ISBN: 979-8-8734-6573-6

Preamble

This recipe book is the fruit of my personal experience and passion for healthy, low-glycemic eating. I would like to make it clear that I am not a doctor, nutritionist or dietician. The information provided in this book is based on my own research, culinary experience and knowledge acquired over time.

It is important to note that each individual has unique nutritional needs, and this book is not a substitute for professional medical advice. Before making any significant changes to your diet, I strongly recommend that you consult a qualified health professional, such as a doctor, nutritionist or dietician, for personalized advice tailored to your specific situation.

The recipes presented in this book have been developed with the aim of promoting a low glycemic index diet, but it is essential to take into account your own needs, food allergies and health conditions when preparing and eating the dishes suggested.

By using this book, you acknowledge and agree that the author cannot be held responsible for any consequences arising from the use of the recipes or information presented in this book.

Contents

INTRODUCTION

- 1 **Glycemic Index for vegetarians**
- 2 Introduction to low-glycemic diets for vegetarians
- 3 The importance of nutritional balance in a low-GI vegetarian diet
- 4 Practical advice and nutritional tips
- 5 Product typology to facilitate recipe preparation
- 6 Shopping list tips
- 7 Glycemic Index (GI) scale

REVITALIZING BREAKFASTS

- 9 **Smoothies and energy drinks**
- 10 Energizing Smoothie with chia and berries
- 12 Green smoothie refreshing
- 15 Morning vitality smoothie
- 16 Protein smoothie with almond butter
- 18 Antioxidant coconut-banana smoothie
- 20 Detoxifying green smoothie
- 23 Blackberry and fresh mint smoothie
- 24 Oatmeal and red fruit smoothie
- 27 **Fruit and wholegrain bowls**
- 28 Fruit and quinoa energy bowl
- 30 Fruit & wholegrain bowl
- 33 Fibre-rich oatmeal and fruit bowl
- 34 Fresh fruit and barley bowl
- 36 Vitality bowl with millet and fruit
- 39 Antioxidant berry and quinoa bowl
- 40 Fruit and muesli energy bowl
- 43 **Plant-based alternatives to dairy products**
- 44 Vegan yoghurt with vanilla and almonds
- 46 Vegetable cheese with tofu and fresh herbs
- 49 Cashew and wild berry yoghurt
- 50 Vegan fromage blanc with soy yogurt
- 52 Coconut-vanilla whipped cream
- 55 **Seed and nut creations**
- 56 Crunchy granola mix with nuts and fruit
- 59 Energy bars with nuts and dried fruit
- 61 Crunchy nut and seed porridge
- 62 Chia seed and walnut smoothie bowl
- 64 Muesli with nuts, seeds and dried fruit

SATIATING BREAKFASTS

- 67 **Complete and satiating salads**
- 68 Quinoa salad with roasted vegetables
- 70 Mediterranean lentil and vegetable salad
- 72 Roasted chickpea salad with grilled vegetables
- 75 Lentil salad with crunchy vegetables
- 76 Quinoa salad with grilled vegetables
- 79 White bean salad with grilled vegetables
- 80 Quinoa salad with crunchy vegetables
- 82 Brown rice salad with summer vegetables
- 85 **Balanced sandwiches and wraps**
- 86 Grilled vegetable and hummus sandwich
- 88 Grilled vegetable and marinated tofu sandwich
- 91 Legume and guacamole sandwich
- 93 Protein wrap with black beans and avocado
- 94 Roasted vegetable and goat cheese sandwich
- 96 Mediterranean sandwich with grilled vegetables
- 98 Wrap with sautéed mushrooms and chickpea hummus
- 101 **Takeaway lunch options**
- 102 Vegetable quinoa salad for packed lunches
- 104 Crisp vegetable wrap with chickpea spread
- 107 Lentil and vegetable salad for a nomadic lunch
- 108 Wrap with grilled vegetables and feta cheese
- 110 Quinoa salad with vegetables and avocado
- 113 **Vegetarian hot dishes for lunch**
- 114 Pan-fried vegetables with quinoa
- 117 Pasta with grilled vegetables and homemade tomato sauce
- 118 Vegetable and tofu curry
- 121 Chili végétarien aux haricots
- 122 Ratatouille Provençale

TASTY DINNERS

- **125 Legume and whole-grain dishes**
  - 126 Quinoa and black bean bowl
  - 128 Salade de lentilles et boulgour
  - 131 Pan-fried chickpeas and quinoa
  - 132 Lentil and vegetable curry
  - 134 Fried quinoa with vegetables
  - 137 Roasted chickpeas with vegetables
  - 138 Quinoa Galettes with Black Beans
  - 140 Tofu sauté with vegetables and sesame seeds

- **143 Varieties of vegetable dishes and plant proteins**
  - 144 Chickpea and sweet potato curry
  - 146 Ratatouille with white beans
  - 149 Pan-fried vegetables with lentils
  - 151 Tofu and vegetable curry
  - 152 Chickpea and spinach curry
  - 154 Tofu sauté with crunchy vegetables
  - 157 Ratatouille with fresh herbs

- **159 Plant-based alternatives to traditional dishes**
  - 160 Vegetarian vegetable lasagne
  - 162 Winter vegetable and barley fritters
  - 165 Zucchini stuffed with vegetables and quinoa
  - 166 Peppers stuffed with vegetables and brown rice
  - 168 Summer vegetable tart

- **171 Light, balanced dinners**
  - 172 Spinach salad with strawberries and walnuts
  - 174 Pan-fried summer vegetables with grilled tofu
  - 177 Vegetable curry with coconut milk
  - 178 Ratatouille with herbs and quinoa
  - 180 Vegetable and chickpea curry

EXQUISITE DESSERTS

- **183 Sweet options with fresh and dried fruit**
  - 184 Fresh and dried fruit salad with mint
  - 186 Apple compote with dried fruit and cinnamon
  - 189 Winter fruit salad with walnuts
  - 190 Summer fruit carpaccio with almonds
  - 192 Grilled fruit skewers with mint
  - 194 Bowl of Greek yogurt with fruit and nuts
  - 196 Light fruit mousse
  - 198 Exotic fruit salad with coconut

- **201 Light and balanced pastries**
  - 202 Oatmeal and fruit muffins
  - 204 Banana and almond cookies
  - 206 Date and walnut cookies
  - 208 Coconut and almond energy bites
  - 210 Vanilla and almond shortbread cookies
  - 212 Coconut bites with dried fruit
  - 214 Banana and dark chocolate cookies

- **217 Healthy alternatives to satisfy sweet cravings**
  - 218 Coconut and dried fruit energy balls
  - 220 Red fruit and almond cream tartlets
  - 223 Summer fruit chia pudding
  - 224 Greek yogurt with red fruit and almonds
  - 226 Cinnamon applesauce

- **229 Frozen and gourmet desserts**
  - 230 Red fruit and Greek yogurt popsicles
  - 232 Tropical mango and coconut sorbet
  - 235 Watermelon granita
  - 236 Frozen yogurt and berry sticks
  - 238 Lemongrass and mint granita

APPENDICES

- **241 Measurements and ingredients**
  - 242 Table of Glycemic Indexes for common foods
  - 243 Conversion of measures to facilitate book use
  - 243 List of essential low-GI vegetarian ingredients to have in your kitchen

INTRODUCTION

Glycemic Index for vegetarians

Introduction > Glycemic Index for vegetarians

Introduction to low-glycemic diets for vegetarians

The low glycemic index diet is a holistic and balanced approach for vegetarians seeking to optimize their health. Based on controlling the body's glycemic response to food, this method favors food choices that have a moderate impact on blood sugar levels after meals.

For vegetarians, this approach is particularly important. Indeed, by eliminating or limiting animal products, dietary diversity becomes essential to meet nutritional needs, and the glycemic index of foods plays a key role in managing this diversity.

In this context, favouring foods with a low glycemic index helps to regulate blood sugar levels more consistently, thus promoting satiety, reducing insulin spikes and contributing to better body weight control. What's more, this approach can be beneficial in the prevention and management of various health conditions, such as type 2 diabetes or cardiovascular disease.

This cookbook, specially designed for vegetarians, explores a variety of low-glycemic dishes and ingredients, offering a diverse and balanced palette of tastes. Each recipe is carefully crafted to combine flavor, nutrients and glycemic balance, encouraging a healthy lifestyle without compromising on taste satisfaction.

By understanding the fundamentals of low-glycemic eating and learning how to select and cook suitable ingredients, vegetarians can not only diversify their diet, but also improve their overall well-being. This book is a practical and inspiring guide to a nourishing, energizing and body-friendly diet.

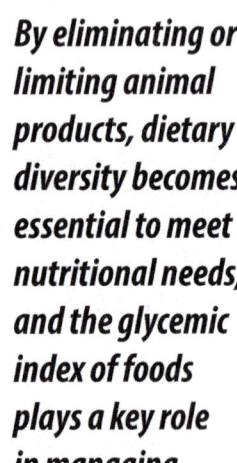

> **By eliminating or limiting animal products, dietary diversity becomes essential to meet nutritional needs, and the glycemic index of foods plays a key role in managing this diversity.**

The importance of nutritional balance in a low-GI vegetarian diet

The importance of nutritional balance in a low-glycemic vegetarian diet is fundamental to ensuring optimal health while meeting the specific nutritional needs of this dietary pattern.

The vegetarian diet, with its exclusion of meat and often fish, requires particular attention to the quality and variety of foods consumed to ensure an adequate intake of protein, essential amino acids, iron, calcium, vitamins B12 and D, among other essential nutrients. Integrating this restriction into a low glycemic index diet requires a thorough understanding of the nutritional value of foods and their impact on blood glucose levels.

Nutritional balance in this context involves the judicious selection of low-glycemic index foods while ensuring that protein, fiber, healthy fats and micronutrient requirements are covered. This can be achieved by including legumes, whole grains, vegetables, fruits with a moderate glycemic index, and a variety of vegetable protein sources such as tofu, tempeh, seeds and nuts.

Maintaining this balance not only ensures stable blood sugar levels, but also promotes satiety, healthy weight, cardiovascular and digestive health, and stable energy throughout the day.

This recipe book aims to present tasty and nutritious food combinations, highlighting low-glycemic food combinations that meet the specific needs of vegetarians.

Nutritional balance in this context involves the judicious selection of foods with a low glycemic index, while ensuring that protein, fiber, healthy fats and micronutrient requirements are covered.

> By understanding and putting into practice these principles of nutritional balance, readers will not only be able to enjoy delicious meals, but also take full advantage of the benefits of both a vegetarian and low-glycemic diet for optimal health.

Introduction > Glycemic Index for vegetarians

Practical advice and nutritional tips

- **Choosing low-GI foods:** Opt for low-GI foods such as green vegetables, legumes, whole grains, fresh fruit and low-fat dairy products. These promote a slow release of glucose into the bloodstream, keeping energy levels stable throughout the day.

- **Balancing meals:** Make sure every meal contains a combination of plant-based proteins, good carbohydrates and healthy fats. This combination promotes satiety and regulates blood sugar levels.

- **Portion management:** Although low-GI foods are beneficial, the quantity consumed is still important. Respecting recommended portions helps maintain nutritional balance.

- **Prefer gentle cooking:** Prefer gentle cooking methods such as steaming, low-temperature cooking or light stir-frying. This preserves nutrients and minimizes the rise in the glycemic index of foods.

- **Good fats count:** Incorporate healthy fats such as those found in avocados, walnuts, flaxseeds and olive oil into your daily diet. They benefit cardiovascular health and contribute to better nutrient absorption.

- **Sugar management:** Reduce your consumption of refined sugar by substituting natural alternatives such as honey, maple syrup or dates to sweeten your preparations.

- **Meal planning:** Plan your meals and snacks in advance to avoid impulsive food choices. This will make it easier for you to maintain your low-GI diet.

- **Adequate hydration:** Drink enough water throughout the day. Sometimes, dehydration can be confused with hunger, which can lead to inappropriate food choices..

> *Meal balancing, portion management, gentle cooking, healthy fats, sugar management, meal planning and proper hydration.*

By incorporating these tips and tricks into your daily routine, you can maximize the benefits of a low-glycemic vegetarian diet, promoting your overall well-being and sustainable energy.

Product typology to facilitate recipe preparation

- **Whole grains and gluten-free alternatives:** Choose from a variety of whole grains such as quinoa, brown rice, oats and buckwheat. For those avoiding gluten, explore gluten-free alternatives such as millet, black rice or teff for dish diversity.

- **Varied legumes:** From lentils and chickpeas to black and kidney beans, these legumes are rich sources of vegetable protein. Opt for dried or canned versions for added convenience in preparation.

- **Fresh and frozen vegetables:** Fill up on fresh seasonal vegetables for nutritional diversity. Frozen vegetables can also be handy for quick recipes and remain just as nutrient-rich.

- **Fresh and dried fruit:** Fresh fruit can be used for desserts or smoothies. Dried fruits such as dates, figs or apricots can be used as natural sugar substitutes in many recipes.

> *You can create tasty, balanced, low-GI meals, promoting better blood sugar management, stable energy and optimal overall health.*

- **Plant-based dairy substitutes:** Opt for almond, soy, coconut or oat milk instead of cow's milk. Plant-based yoghurt and cheeses also offer flavor-rich alternatives.

- **Seeds and nuts:** Incorporate chia seeds, flax seeds, pumpkin seeds or nuts such as almonds, hazelnuts or cashews into your dishes to add interesting textures and extra nutritional benefits.

- **Natural sweeteners:** Apart from traditional sugar, explore natural sweeteners such as maple syrup, honey, agave syrup or dates to sweeten your preparations in a healthier way.

- **Spices and herbs:** Vary flavors by using a palette of spices and herbs. From turmeric and paprika to thyme and basil, these ingredients add depth of flavour without compromising health..

> By incorporating these products into your pantry, you'll have a varied and versatile base from which to prepare a wide range of low-glycemic vegetarian recipes with ease and creativity.

Introduction > **Glycemic Index for vegetarians**

Shopping list tips

- **Weekly meal planning:** Before drawing up your shopping list, draw up a weekly menu. This will help you determine exactly what ingredients you need for each meal, thus minimizing food waste.

- **Prioritize fresh, in-season foods:** Fresh, in-season produce is not only tastier, but often less expensive. Consult the seasonal produce calendars to guide you in your choices.

- **Maintain diversity:** Be sure to include a variety of foods to ensure a balanced nutritional intake. Add different-colored vegetables, varied sources of vegetable protein and whole grains to your list.

- **Check supplies before you go:** Before you go shopping, take a look at what you already have in your pantry. This will help you avoid buying items you already have, and will help you complete your list more accurately.

- **Flexibility in substitutes:** If a specific ingredient isn't available, plan for alternative substitutes. For example, if one type of bean isn't available, opt for another similar variety.

- **Avoid impulse buys:** Stick to your list as much as possible to avoid impulse buys. These purchases can lead to food waste and deviate from your intended nutritional choices.

- **Use apps or digital lists:** Shopping list apps can be handy for keeping track of what you need. Some even allow you to check off items as you add them to your basket.

- **Regularly re-evaluate your habits:** Finally, regularly re-evaluate your shopping lists and menu to adjust your needs according to your lifestyle and changing food preferences..

> By following these tips, your shopping lists will become effective tools to help you maintain a balanced diet and prepare low-glycemic vegetarian meals, without stress or waste.

Glycemic Index (GI) scale

The Glycemic Index (GI) scale ranks foods on a scale from 0 to 100, according to how quickly they raise blood sugar levels after consumption. Here's how this scale is generally divided:

- **Low GI (0-55):** Foods with a low GI cause a slow, moderate rise in blood sugar (legumes, certain fruits, unsweetened dairy products, etc.).

- **Medium GI (56-69):** Foods with a medium GI have a moderate to high impact on blood sugar levels (certain varieties of rice, pasta, etc.).

- **High GI (70 and over):** Foods with a high GI cause a rapid and significant rise in blood sugar levels (sweets, white bread, potatoes, etc.).

However, it's important to note that GI can vary depending on a number of factors, such as food preparation, the combination of foods in a meal, and the way foods are cooked. This classification can be a useful guide to choosing foods that help maintain stable blood sugar levels, but other dietary factors must also be taken into account for a healthy, balanced diet.

For more details, see the **Table of Glycemic Indexes for common foods** in the appendix, page 242.

REVITALIZING BREAKFASTS

Smoothies and energy drinks

ENERGIZING SMOOTHIE WITH CHIA AND BERRIES

SERVINGS

For 2 persons

PREPARATION TIME

10 minutes

INGREDIENTS

- ✔ 2 tablespoons chia seeds
- ✔ 1 cup mixed berries (strawberries, raspberries, blueberries)
- ✔ 1 ripe banana (medium GI)
- ✔ 1 cup unsweetened almond milk
- ✔ 1 tablespoon almond butter
- ✔ 1 teaspoon honey or maple syrup (optional, low GI: moderate)
- ✔ A few ice cubes

INSTRUCTIONS

1. In a bowl, mix the chia seeds with the almond milk. Leave to stand for 5 – 10 minutes so that the chia seeds swell and form a gel.
2. Meanwhile, peel and chop the banana.
3. In a blender, add the mixed berries, banana, almond butter and honey or maple syrup.
4. Pour the mixture of chia seeds and almond milk into the blender.
5. Add a few ice cubes for a fresher, creamier texture.
6. Blend until smooth and homogenous.
7. Taste and adjust the sweetness by adding a little more honey or maple syrup if necessary.

> Pour the energizing chia-berry smoothie into tall glasses. Decorate the top with a few fresh berries or mint leaves. Serve with a reusable straw for an elegant presentation.

GREEN SMOOTHIE REFRESHING

SERVINGS

For 2 persons

PREPARATION TIME

7 minutes

INGREDIENTS

- ✔ 2 cups fresh baby spinach
- ✔ 1 ripe avocado
- ✔ ½ cucumber
- ✔ 1 green apple, seeded and chopped
- ✔ ½ lemon, freshly squeezed
- ✔ 1 cup unsweetened coconut water
- ✔ A few ice cubes

INSTRUCTIONS

1. Thoroughly wash the baby spinach and cucumber. Peel the avocado and remove the stone. Cut all ingredients into pieces to facilitate blending.
2. In a blender, add baby spinach, avocado, cucumber, chopped green apple, lemon juice and coconut water.
3. Add a few ice cubes for a cooler, more refreshing consistency.
4. Blend all ingredients until smooth and creamy.

> Serve the refreshing green smoothie in smoothie glasses. You can decorate the rim of the glasses with a cucumber slice or mint leaf for a visual touch. For an even more elegant presentation, use reusable straws.

MORNING VITALITY SMOOTHIE

SERVINGS

For 2 persons

PREPARATION TIME

5 minutes

INGREDIENTS

- ✔ 2 oranges, peeled and quartered (GI: 40)
- ✔ 1 ripe banana (GI: 51)
- ✔ 1 cup baby spinach leaves
- ✔ 1 tablespoon ground flaxseed
- ✔ 1 cup coconut water
- ✔ A few ice cubes (optional)

INSTRUCTIONS

1. Place the orange segments, banana, spinach shoots and flaxseed in a blender.
2. Pour coconut water into blender.
3. Add ice cubes if you prefer a colder texture.
4. Blend until smooth.

Serve the berry-oat smoothie in smoothie glasses decorated with fresh berries around the rim. You can sprinkle a pinch of oatmeal on top for a rustic presentation.

PROTEIN SMOOTHIE WITH ALMOND BUTTER

SERVINGS

For 2 persons

PREPARATION TIME

5 minutes

INGREDIENTS

- ✔ 2 tablespoons unsweetened vegetable protein powder
- ✔ 2 tablespoons almond butter
- ✔ 1 ripe banana (medium GI)
- ✔ 1 cup unsweetened almond milk
- ✔ 1 cup fresh spinach
- ✔ 1 teaspoon cinnamon powder
- ✔ A few ice cubes

INSTRUCTIONS

1. Place the vegetable protein powder, almond butter, banana, almond milk, spinach and cinnamon in a blender.
2. Add a few ice cubes for a more refreshing texture.
3. Blend all ingredients until smooth and creamy.

Pour the almond butter protein smoothie into smoothie glasses. Sprinkle cinnamon lightly over the top for a touch of color and flavor. You can also add a few slivered almonds for a crunchy presentation.

ANTIOXIDANT COCONUT-BANANA SMOOTHIE

SERVINGS

For 2 persons

PREPARATION TIME

7 minutes

INGREDIENTS

- 1 ripe banana (medium GI)
- 1 cup unsweetened coconut milk
- 1 cup baby spinach
- ½ cup fresh or frozen pineapple chunks
- 1 tablespoon hemp seeds
- 1 tablespoon unsweetened shredded coconut
- A few ice cubes

INSTRUCTIONS

1. Place the banana, coconut milk, baby spinach, pineapple, hemp seeds and shredded coconut in a blender.
2. Add a few ice cubes for a fresher texture.
3. Blend all ingredients until smooth and homogeneous.

> Pour the antioxidant coconut-banana smoothie into smoothie glasses. Garnish the top of the smoothie with a little shredded coconut or a few pineapple pieces for a tropical presentation.

DETOXIFYING GREEN SMOOTHIE

SERVINGS

For 2 persons

PREPARATION TIME

8 minutes

INGREDIENTS

- ✔ 2 cups kale or kale seed
- ✔ 1 green apple, cored and chopped
- ✔ 1 medium cucumber, peeled and chopped
- ✔ 1 stalk celery, chopped
- ✔ ½ lemon, freshly squeezed
- ✔ 1 1-inch piece fresh ginger, peeled and chopped
- ✔ 1 cup unsweetened coconut water
- ✔ A few ice cubes

INSTRUCTIONS

1. Thoroughly wash the kale, apple, cucumber and celery.
2. Place the kale, green apple, cucumber, celery, lemon juice, fresh ginger and coconut water in a blender.
3. Add a few ice cubes for a fresher texture.
4. Blend all ingredients to a smooth, creamy consistency.

> Serve the detoxifying green smoothie in smoothie glasses. Garnish with a slice of cucumber or a leaf of kale for an attractive presentation.

BLACKBERRY AND FRESH MINT SMOOTHIE

SERVINGS

For 2 persons

PREPARATION TIME

5 minutes

INGREDIENTS

- ✔ 2 cups fresh or frozen blackberries
- ✔ ½ cup plain Greek yogurt
- ✔ 1 cup unsweetened almond milk
- ✔ A few fresh mint leaves
- ✔ 1 tablespoon chia seeds
- ✔ 1 tablespoon honey or maple syrup (optional, low GI: moderate)
- ✔ A few ice cubes

INSTRUCTIONS

1. In a blender, add the blackberries, Greek yogurt, almond milk and fresh mint leaves.
2. Add chia seeds for a touch of texture and extra nutrients.
3. If desired, add honey or maple syrup for extra sweetness.
4. Add a few ice cubes for a refreshing consistency.
5. Blend until smooth and creamy.

Pour the blackberry and fresh mint smoothie into smoothie glasses. Decorate with a few fresh blackberries on top and a mint leaf for a colorful, aromatic presentation.

OATMEAL AND RED FRUIT SMOOTHIE

SERVINGS

For 2 persons

PREPARATION TIME

7 minutes

INGREDIENTS

- 1 cup unsweetened almond milk
- ½ cup rolled oats
- 1 cup mixed berries (strawberries, raspberries, blueberries)
- 1 ripe banana (medium GI)
- 1 tablespoon ground flaxseed
- 1 tablespoon honey or maple syrup (optional, low GI: moderate)
- A few ice cubes

INSTRUCTIONS

1. Pour the almond milk and rolled oats into a blender. Soak for a few minutes to soften the flakes.
2. Add the berries, banana, ground flax seeds and honey or maple syrup.
3. Add a few ice cubes for a fresher texture.
4. Blend all ingredients to a smooth, creamy consistency.

Serve the oat-red fruit smoothie in smoothie glasses. Decorate with a few berries around the rim or a sprinkling of oatmeal on top for a visually appealing presentation.

REVITALIZING BREAKFASTS
Fruit and wholegrain bowls

FRUIT AND QUINOA ENERGY BOWL

SERVINGS

For 2 persons

PREPARATION TIME

15 minutes

COOKING TIME

15 minutes

INGREDIENTS

- 1 cup cooked quinoa
- 1 ripe banana (medium GI)
- 1 cup strawberries, quartered
- ½ cup fresh blueberries
- 2 tablespoons chia seeds
- 2 tablespoons chopped walnuts
- 1 tablespoon maple syrup or honey (optional, low GI: moderate)
- Plain Greek yoghurt for garnish

INSTRUCTIONS

1. Cook quinoa according to package instructions. Leave to cool.
2. Divide the cooked quinoa between two bowls.
3. Add the banana quarters, chopped strawberries, blueberries and chia seeds on top of the quinoa.
4. Sprinkle with chopped walnuts and drizzle with maple syrup or honey if you wish to add a sweet touch.
5. Garnish with a spoonful of Greek yoghurt on top for extra creaminess and protein.

Present the fruit and quinoa energy bowl attractively in bowls. For a visual touch, arrange the fruit and seeds harmoniously on top. You can lightly sprinkle with additional crushed nuts for a crunchy, appetizing presentation.

FRUIT & WHOLEGRAIN BOWL

SERVINGS

For 2 persons

PREPARATION TIME

10 minutes

INGREDIENTS

- 1 cup plain Greek yogurt
- 1 ripe banana, sliced into rounds
- 1 cup fresh strawberries, chopped
- ½ cup rolled oats
- 2 tablespoons chia seeds
- 2 tablespoons pumpkin seeds
- A few chopped walnuts or almonds
- 1 tablespoon honey or maple syrup (low GI, optional)
- A few mint leaves for garnish (optional)

INSTRUCTIONS

1. Divide the Greek yogurt between two bowls.
2. Add banana slices and strawberry pieces to the yoghurt in each bowl.
3. Sprinkle the oats, chia seeds and pumpkin seeds evenly over the fruit.
4. If desired, drizzle with a tablespoon of honey or maple syrup to sweeten slightly.
5. Sprinkle with crushed walnuts or almonds for extra crunch.
6. Garnish with mint leaves for a touch of freshness.

Serve these bowls of fresh, colorful fruit and wholegrain cereals. Present them beautifully, with a careful arrangement of ingredients to highlight the different layers. You can also offer a few extra slices of fruit on top for a more elaborate presentation.

FIBRE-RICH OATMEAL AND FRUIT BOWL

SERVINGS

For 2 persons

PREPARATION TIME

10 minutes

INGREDIENTS

- 1 cup cooked rolled oats
- 1 ripe banana (medium GI)
- ½ cup mixed berries (strawberries, raspberries, blueberries)
- ¼ cup pomegranate seeds
- 2 tablespoons chopped walnuts
- 1 tablespoon sunflower seeds
- 1 tablespoon maple syrup or honey (optional, low GI: moderate)
- Vegan yoghurt for garnish

INSTRUCTIONS

1. Divide the cooked oatmeal between two breakfast bowls.
2. Slice the banana and arrange it on top of the oatmeal in the bowls.
3. Add the mixed berries and pomegranate seeds on top of the oats and banana.
4. Sprinkle crushed walnuts and sunflower seeds over the fruit.
5. Drizzle with maple syrup or honey for extra sweetness if desired.
6. Top each bowl with a spoonful of plant-based yoghurt for a creamy texture.

Present the fiber-rich bowls with oatmeal and fruit attractively on a table. Arrange the fruit and seeds aesthetically for a colorful, appetizing presentation. Add a finishing touch by sprinkling a few extra sunflower seeds on top.

FRESH FRUIT AND BARLEY BOWL

SERVINGS

For 2 persons

PREPARATION TIME

15 minutes

INGREDIENTS

- 1 cup cooked barley
- 1 ripe banana (medium GI)
- 1 cup diced fresh pineapple
- ½ cup kiwi slices
- 2 tablespoons poppy seeds
- 2 tablespoons chopped cashews
- 1 tablespoon agave syrup or honey (optional, low GI: moderate)
- Vegan yoghurt for garnish

INSTRUCTIONS

1. Divide the cooked barley between two bowls.
2. Slice the banana and arrange on top of the barley in the bowls.
3. Divide the pineapple cubes and kiwi slices between the barley and banana.
4. Sprinkle poppy seeds and crushed cashews over the fruit.
5. Add agave syrup or honey to sweeten slightly if desired.
6. Top each bowl with a spoonful of plant-based yoghurt for a creamy touch.

Present fresh fruit and barley bowls attractively on a table. Arrange the fruit and seeds harmoniously for a visually pleasing presentation. Sprinkle with additional poppy seeds for a touch of texture.

VITALITY BOWL WITH MILLET AND FRUIT

SERVINGS

For 2 persons

PREPARATION TIME

20 minutes

INGREDIENTS

- 1 cup cooked millet
- 1 ripe banana (medium GI)
- 1 cup diced fresh mango
- ½ cup strawberry slices
- 2 tablespoons sesame seeds
- 2 tablespoons chopped pecans
- 1 tablespoon maple syrup or honey (optional, low GI: moderate)
- Vegan yoghurt for garnish

INSTRUCTIONS

1. Divide the cooked millet between two bowls.
2. Slice the banana and arrange on top of the millet in the bowls.
3. Divide the diced mango and strawberry slices between the millet and banana.
4. Sprinkle sesame seeds and crushed pecans over the fruit.
5. Add a drizzle of maple syrup or honey for extra sweetness if desired.
6. Top each bowl with a spoonful of plant-based yoghurt for a creamy texture.

> Present the millet and fruit vitality bowls artistically on a table. Arrange the fruit and seeds for an attractive aesthetic. For a finishing touch, sprinkle extra sesame seeds lightly over the top.

Revitalizing breakfasts > **Fruit and wholegrain bowls** | 39

ANTIOXIDANT BERRY AND QUINOA BOWL

SERVINGS

For 2 persons

PREPARATION TIME

15 minutes

INGREDIENTS

- 1 cup cooked quinoa
- 1 ripe banana (medium GI)
- 1 cup fresh blueberries
- ½ cup fresh raspberries
- 2 tablespoons pomegranate seeds
- 2 tablespoons slivered almonds
- 1 tablespoon maple syrup or honey (optional, low GI: moderate)
- Vegan yoghurt for garnish

INSTRUCTIONS

1. Divide the cooked quinoa between two bowls.
2. Slice the banana and arrange on top of the quinoa in the bowls.
3. Scatter the blueberries and raspberries over the quinoa and banana.
4. Sprinkle pomegranate seeds and flaked almonds over the fruit.
5. Add a drizzle of maple syrup or honey for a sweet touch, if desired.
6. Top each bowl with a spoonful of plant-based yoghurt for a creamy texture.

Present antioxidant berry and quinoa bowls neatly on a table. Arrange the fruits and seeds for a visually appealing presentation. For a finishing touch, sprinkle extra flaked almonds lightly over the top.

FRUIT AND MUESLI ENERGY BOWL

SERVINGS

For 2 persons

PREPARATION TIME

10 minutes

INGREDIENTS

- 1 cup plain Greek yogurt
- 1 green apple, diced
- 1 cup mixed berries (strawberries, blueberries, raspberries - low GI)
- ½ cup no-sugar-added muesli
- 2 tablespoons flax seeds
- 2 tablespoons slivered almonds
- 1 tablespoon honey or maple syrup (low GI, optional)
- A few fresh basil leaves for garnish (optional)

INSTRUCTIONS

1. Divide the Greek yogurt between two bowls.
2. Arrange the diced green apple and mixed berries over the yoghurt in each bowl.
3. Sprinkle the muesli over the fruit in the bowls.
4. Add flax seeds and slivered almonds for a crunchy texture.
5. If desired, drizzle with a tablespoon of honey or maple syrup to sweeten slightly.
6. Garnish with a few fresh basil leaves for an aromatic touch.

Present these fruit and muesli energy bowls with an artistic arrangement of ingredients to highlight each layer. You can also add a few extra pieces of fruit on top for a more elaborate presentation.

REVITALIZING BREAKFASTS

Plant-based alternatives to dairy products

VEGAN YOGHURT WITH VANILLA AND ALMONDS

SERVINGS

Serves 4

PREPARATION TIME

10 minutes

INGREDIENTS

- ✓ 2 cups unsweetened almond milk
- ✓ 1 cup almond cream
- ✓ 2 tablespoons maple or agave syrup (optional, low GI: moderate)
- ✓ 1 vanilla pod or 1 teaspoon vanilla extract
- ✓ 1 tablespoon chia seeds
- ✓ Fresh fruit for garnish (strawberries, blueberries, etc.)

INSTRUCTIONS

1. Mix the almond milk and cream in a bowl.
2. If you're using a vanilla pod, split it open and scrape out the seeds. Add the vanilla seeds or vanilla extract to the mixture.
3. Add the chia seeds to thicken the mixture. Mix well.
4. If you prefer your yoghurt slightly sweetened, add maple or agave syrup to taste.
5. Divide the mixture between individual bowls or jars.
6. Leave in the fridge for at least 2 hours to allow the chia seeds to thicken the yoghurt.
7. Just before serving, garnish with fresh fruit.

> Serve the vanilla-almond vegetable yoghurt in individual bowls. Garnish with a handful of fresh fruit on top for a contrast of colors and flavors. You can also sprinkle lightly with chia seeds or slivered almonds for a textured presentation.

VEGETABLE CHEESE WITH TOFU AND FRESH HERBS

SERVINGS

Serves 4

PREPARATION TIME

15 minutes

INGREDIENTS

- 400 g firm tofu, drained
- Juice of half a lemon
- 2 tablespoons nutritional yeast
- 1 teaspoon garlic powder
- 1 teaspoon onion powder
- 1 tablespoon chopped fresh herbs (parsley, chives, basil)
- Salt and pepper to taste

INSTRUCTIONS

1. 400 g firm tofu, drained
2. Juice of half a lemon
3. 2 tablespoons nutritional yeast
4. 1 teaspoon garlic powder
5. 1 teaspoon onion powder
6. 1 tablespoon chopped fresh herbs (parsley, chives, basil)
7. Salt and pepper to taste

Serve the vegetable cheese with tofu and fresh herbs in individual ramekins. Decorate with a few extra fresh herbs on top for a colorful presentation. Serve with slices of wholemeal bread or fresh vegetables for spreading.

CASHEW AND WILD BERRY YOGHURT

SERVINGS

Serves 4

PREPARATION TIME

10 minutes (+ soaking time)

INGREDIENTS

- 1 cup raw cashews (soaked for at least 4 hours)
- 1 cup filtered water
- 1 tablespoon maple or agave syrup (optional, low GI: moderate)
- 1 teaspoon vanilla extract
- 1 cup mixed berries (strawberries, blueberries, raspberries)

INSTRUCTIONS

1. After soaking the cashews, drain and rinse thoroughly.
2. In a powerful blender, combine the drained cashews, filtered water, maple or agave syrup (if using) and vanilla extract.
3. Blend until smooth and creamy, scraping down the sides of the blender if necessary.
4. Divide the cashew yoghurt between individual bowls or dishes.
5. Garnish with mixed berries.

Serve the cashew and berry yoghurt in individual bowls. Arrange the berries on top for a colorful, appetizing presentation. Sprinkle with a few crushed cashews for a crunchy touch.

VEGAN FROMAGE BLANC WITH SOY YOGURT

SERVINGS

Serves 4

PREPARATION TIME

10 minutes (+ rest time)

INGREDIENTS

- 500 g plain unsweetened soy yoghurt
- Juice of half a lemon
- 1 tablespoon cider vinegar
- 1 tablespoon nutritional yeast
- 1 pinch salt

INSTRUCTIONS

1. In a bowl, mix the soy yogurt with the lemon juice, cider vinegar, nutritional yeast and salt.
2. Mix all ingredients until smooth and homogeneous.
3. Leave the mixture to rest in the fridge for at least 2 hours to allow the flavors to develop.

> Serve soy yogurt fromage blanc in individual bowls or on a serving platter. Serve with fresh fruit, dried fruit or nuts for a varied and colorful presentation.

COCONUT-VANILLA WHIPPED CREAM

SERVINGS

Serves 4

PREPARATION TIME

10 minutes (+ refrigeration time)

INGREDIENTS

- 1 can coconut milk, chilled for at least 8 hours
- 1 tablespoon maple or agave syrup (optional, low GI: moderate)
- 1 teaspoon vanilla extract

INSTRUCTIONS

1. Place the can of coconut milk in the refrigerator for at least 8 hours or overnight.
2. Remove the refrigerated can of coconut milk from the fridge. Be careful not to shake the can.
3. Open the can and carefully remove the solid part of the coconut milk that has separated from the liquid.
4. Place the solid part of the coconut milk in a bowl.
5. Add the maple or agave syrup (if using) and vanilla extract.
6. Using an electric mixer, whip the mixture to a creamy consistency.
7. Refrigerate the whipped cream for about 30 minutes before serving.

Serve coconut-vanilla whipped cream in individual bowls or cups. Use it with fresh fruit or desserts for a creamy, fragrant addition.

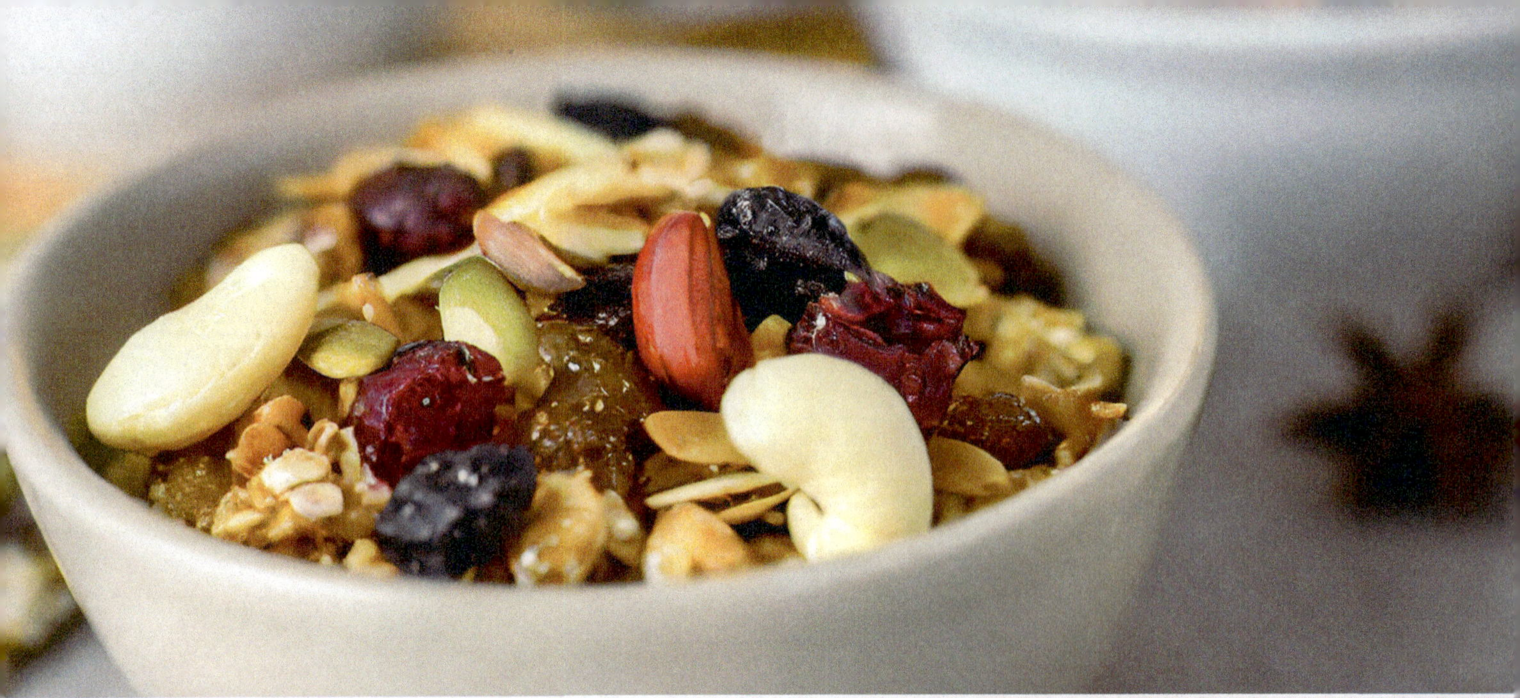
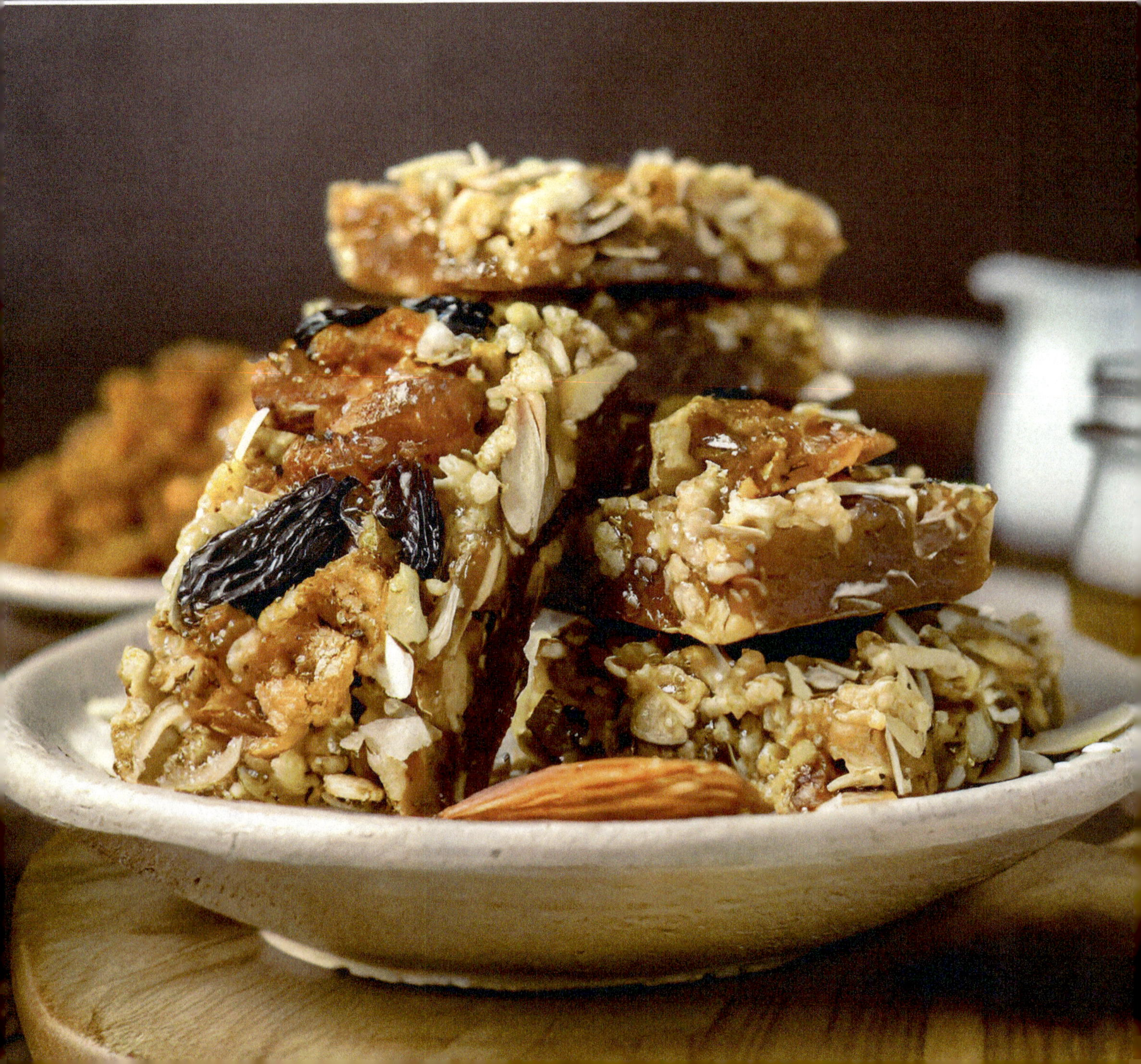

REVITALIZING BREAKFASTS

Seed and nut creations

CRUNCHY GRANOLA MIX WITH NUTS AND FRUIT

SERVINGS

Serves 6

PREPARATION TIME

10 minutes

COOKING TIME

25 minutes

INGREDIENTS

- ✔ 2 cups rolled oats
- ✔ ½ cup slivered almonds
- ✔ ½ cup chopped cashews
- ✔ ¼ cup sunflower seeds
- ✔ ¼ cup pumpkin seeds
- ✔ ¼ cup maple or agave syrup (low GI: moderate)
- ✔ 2 tablespoons coconut oil
- ✔ ½ cup dried cranberries
- ✔ ½ cup raisins
- ✔ 1 teaspoon vanilla extract

INSTRUCTIONS

1. Preheat your oven to 160°C (320°F) and line a baking sheet with parchment paper.
2. In a large bowl, combine the rolled oats, slivered almonds, cashews, sunflower seeds and pumpkin seeds.
3. In a saucepan, heat the maple or agave syrup with the coconut oil and vanilla extract until the mixture is liquid.
4. Pour the liquid mixture over the dry ingredients and mix well to coat evenly.
5. Spread the mixture on the prepared baking sheet and bake for 25 minutes, stirring gently halfway through to ensure even browning.
6. Once golden and crisp, remove from the oven and leave to cool.
7. Add the dried cranberries and raisins to the cooled mixture.

Serve this homemade granola in individual bowls or glass jars for a convenient breakfast. Serve with plant-based yoghurt or plant-based milk for a crunchy, energizing breakfast.

ENERGY BARS WITH NUTS AND DRIED FRUIT

SERVINGS

For 8 bars

PREPARATION TIME

15 minutes

COOKING TIME

20 minutes

INGREDIENTS

- 1 cup rolled oats
- ½ cup shredded coconut
- ½ cup chopped cashews
- ½ cup flaked almonds
- ½ cup sunflower seeds
- ½ cup raisins
- ½ cup pitted dates
- ¼ cup maple or agave syrup (low GI: moderate)
- 2 tablespoons coconut oil
- 1 teaspoon vanilla extract
- Pinch of salt

INSTRUCTIONS

1. Preheat your oven to 160°C (320°F) and line a rectangular baking tin with parchment paper.
2. In a food processor, blend the pitted dates with the maple or agave syrup, coconut oil, vanilla extract and pinch of salt until smooth.
3. In a large bowl, mix the rolled oats, shredded coconut, crushed cashews, slivered almonds, sunflower seeds and raisins.
4. Add the date paste to this dry mixture and mix until all ingredients are well combined.
5. Transfer this mixture to the rectangular tin and press firmly to compact.
6. Bake for about 20 minutes, until the top is golden.
7. Cool completely before cutting into bars.

> Arrange Nut & Dried Fruit Energy Bars on a plate or tray. They can be eaten as they are or individually wrapped for a breakfast or snack to go.

CRUNCHY NUT AND SEED PORRIDGE

SERVINGS

For 2 persons

PREPARATION TIME

5 minutes

COOKING TIME

10 minutes

INGREDIENTS

- 1 cup rolled oats
- 2 cups unsweetened almond milk
- ¼ cup chopped pecans
- 2 tablespoons chia seeds
- 2 tablespoons flax seeds
- 2 tablespoons pumpkin seeds
- 2 tablespoons maple or agave syrup (low GI: moderate)
- Fresh fruit for garnish (banana, berries, etc.)

INSTRUCTIONS

1. Bring the almond milk to the boil in a saucepan.
2. Add the oats and reduce the heat. Simmer for 5 – 7 minutes, stirring regularly, until the porridge thickens.
3. Meanwhile, in a frying pan, lightly toast the crushed pecans, chia seeds, flax seeds and pumpkin seeds over low heat for a few minutes.
4. When the porridge is ready, remove from the heat and add the maple or agave syrup. Mix well.
5. Divide the porridge between bowls.
6. Sprinkle the nut and toasted seed mixture over the porridge.
7. Garnish with fresh fruit.

> Serve the Crunchy Nut & Seed Porridge in individual bowls. Arrange the fresh fruit on top for added freshness and color. You can also add a spoonful of vegetable yoghurt for a creamy touch.

CHIA SEED AND WALNUT SMOOTHIE BOWL

SERVINGS

For 2 persons

PREPARATION TIME

10 minutes

INGREDIENTS

For the smoothie

- ✔ 2 frozen bananas, cut into pieces (medium GI)
- ✔ 1 cup mixed berries (strawberries, blueberries, raspberries)
- ✔ 1 cup unsweetened almond milk
- ✔ 2 tablespoons chia seeds
- ✔ 2 tablespoons nut butter (almond, peanut, etc.)

For the trim

- ✔ Crushed nuts (almonds, walnuts, hazelnuts)
- ✔ Sliced fresh fruit (banana, kiwi, etc.)
- ✔ Shredded coconut flakes
- ✔ Pumpkin and sunflower seeds
- ✔ Honey or maple syrup (optional, low GI: moderate)

INSTRUCTIONS

1. In a blender, combine frozen bananas, mixed berries, almond milk, chia seeds and nut butter. Blend until smooth and creamy.
2. Pour the smoothie into bowls.
3. Add toppings: scatter the crushed walnuts, fresh fruit slices, shredded coconut flakes and pumpkin and sunflower seeds over the smoothie.
4. For an extra touch of sweetness, add a drizzle of honey or maple syrup.

> Carefully decorate the smoothie bowl by artistically arranging the various toppings. Line up slices of fresh fruit or sprinkle evenly with crushed nuts for an attractive presentation. Serve immediately.

MUESLI WITH NUTS, SEEDS AND DRIED FRUIT

SERVINGS

Serves 4

PREPARATION TIME

10 minutes

INGREDIENTS

- ✔ 2 cups rolled oats
- ✔ ½ cup slivered almonds
- ✔ ½ cup chopped pecans
- ✔ ¼ cup sunflower seeds
- ✔ ¼ cup flax seeds
- ✔ ¼ cup raisins
- ✔ ¼ cup dried cranberries
- ✔ ¼ cup diced dried apricots
- ✔ 2 tablespoons maple or agave syrup (low GI: moderate)
- ✔ 2 tablespoons coconut oil
- ✔ 1 teaspoon cinnamon powder

INSTRUCTIONS

1. Preheat your oven to 160°C (320°F) and line a baking sheet with parchment paper.
2. In a large bowl, combine the rolled oats, slivered almonds, crushed pecans, sunflower seeds, flax seeds, raisins, dried cranberries and diced dried apricots.
3. In a saucepan, lightly heat the maple or agave syrup with the coconut oil and cinnamon powder until the mixture is liquid.
4. Pour this liquid mixture over the dry ingredients and mix well to coat evenly.
5. Spread the mixture on the prepared baking sheet and bake for 20 – 25 minutes, stirring gently halfway through to ensure even browning.
6. Once golden and crisp, remove from the oven and allow to cool completely before transferring to an airtight jar.

> Serve this muesli with nuts, seeds and dried fruit in individual bowls with plant-based yoghurt or plant-based milk for a crunchy, nutritious breakfast.

SATIATING BREAKFASTS

Complete and satiating salads

QUINOA SALAD WITH ROASTED VEGETABLES

SERVINGS

Serves 4

PREPARATION TIME

15 minutes

COOKING TIME

25 minutes

INGREDIENTS

- ✔ 1 cup raw quinoa
- ✔ 2 cups water
- ✔ 2 medium zucchini, sliced into rounds
- ✔ 2 red peppers, diced
- ✔ 1 red onion, thinly sliced
- ✔ 2 garlic cloves, chopped
- ✔ 2 tablespoons olive oil
- ✔ Salt and pepper to taste
- ✔ 1 avocado, sliced
- ✔ ¼ cup cherry tomatoes, halved
- ✔ ¼ cup crumbled feta cheese (optional)
- ✔ Juice of one lemon
- ✔ Fresh coriander leaves for garnish

INSTRUCTIONS

1. Preheat oven to 200°C (390°F).
2. In a saucepan, rinse the quinoa in cold water. Add to 2 cups of water, bring to the boil, then reduce heat to low. Simmer for 15 – 20 minutes, until the quinoa absorbs the water. Remove from the heat, cover and leave to rest for 5 minutes, then remove the seeds with a fork.
3. Meanwhile, arrange the zucchini slices, diced red bell pepper, chopped onion and minced garlic on a baking sheet. Drizzle with olive oil and season with salt and pepper. Roast in the oven for around 25 minutes, until the vegetables are tender and lightly browned.
4. In a large bowl, mix the cooked quinoa with the roasted vegetables.
5. Add avocado slices, cherry tomatoes and crumbled feta (if using). Sprinkle with lemon juice.
6. Toss gently and garnish with fresh coriander leaves.

Serve Quinoa Salad with Roasted Vegetables in bowls or on individual plates. For an extra touch, sprinkle sesame seeds or crushed walnuts on top. This salad can be served either warm or cold, depending on your preferences.

MEDITERRANEAN LENTIL AND VEGETABLE SALAD

SERVINGS

Serves 4

PREPARATION TIME

15 minutes

COOKING TIME

25 minutes

INGREDIENTS

- 1 cup cooked green lentils
- 2 zucchini, diced
- 1 yellow bell pepper, diced
- 1 red onion, thinly sliced
- 2 cloves garlic, chopped
- 2 tablespoons olive oil
- Salt and pepper to taste
- 100 g crumbled feta cheese (optional, low GI)
- ¼ cup sun-dried tomatoes, chopped
- Fresh basil leaves for garnish

INSTRUCTIONS

1. Cook green lentils according to package instructions. Drain and set aside.
2. Preheat oven to 200°C (390°F).
3. Place the diced zucchini, diced yellow bell pepper, chopped onion and minced garlic on a baking sheet. Drizzle with olive oil and season with salt and pepper. Mix to coat the vegetables.
4. Roast in the oven for around 20 – 25 minutes, until the vegetables are tender and lightly browned.
5. In a large bowl, mix the cooked lentils with the roasted vegetables.
6. Add the crumbled feta (if using) and sun-dried tomatoes. Mix gently.
7. Garnish with fresh basil leaves before serving.

> Serve this Mediterranean lentil and vegetable salad on individual plates or in bowls. You can accompany this salad with a light vinaigrette of olive oil, lemon and herbs for added flavor. Delicious as a starter or main course.

ROASTED CHICKPEA SALAD WITH GRILLED VEGETABLES

SERVINGS

Serves 4

PREPARATION TIME

15 minutes

COOKING TIME

30 minutes

INGREDIENTS

- 2 cans chickpeas, drained and rinsed (low GI: approx. 28)
- 2 peppers (red and yellow), cut into strips
- 1 zucchini, sliced into rounds
- 1 eggplant, diced
- 1 red onion, thinly sliced
- 2 garlic cloves, minced
- 4 tablespoons olive oil
- 1 teaspoon paprika
- 1 teaspoon cumin powder
- Salt and ground black pepper
- 200 g arugula or mixed baby greens

INSTRUCTIONS

1. Preheat oven to 200°C (gas mark 6-7).
2. In a large ovenproof dish, combine the drained chickpeas, peppers, zucchini, eggplant, red onion and garlic.
3. Drizzle the mixture with olive oil and sprinkle with paprika, cumin, salt and pepper. Mix well to coat all the vegetables.
4. Spread the mixture on a parchment-lined baking sheet and bake for around 25 – 30 minutes, until the vegetables are tender and lightly browned.
5. Meanwhile, arrange the arugula or sprout mixture in a large salad bowl.
6. When the roasted vegetables are ready, let them cool slightly, then add them to the arugula in the salad bowl.

> Serve the roasted chickpea and roasted vegetable salad in individual bowls or on plates. For a finishing touch, sprinkle with toasted sesame seeds or fresh coriander leaves. Serve with a light vinaigrette of lemon juice and olive oil for even more flavor.

LENTIL SALAD WITH CRUNCHY VEGETABLES

SERVINGS

Serves 4

PREPARATION TIME

15 minutes

COOKING TIME

25 minutes

INGREDIENTS

- 1 cup cooked lentils
- 1 cucumber, diced
- 2 carrots, grated
- 1 red bell pepper, diced
- 1 red onion, thinly sliced
- ¼ cup chopped fresh parsley
- ¼ cup balsamic vinegar
- 3 tablespoons olive oil
- 1 teaspoon Dijon mustard
- Salt and pepper to taste
- Sesame seeds for garnish

INSTRUCTIONS

1. Cook lentils according to package instructions. Drain and allow to cool.
2. In a large salad bowl, combine the cooked lentils, cucumber, grated carrots, red bell pepper, red onion and parsley.
3. In a separate bowl, prepare the vinaigrette by mixing the balsamic vinegar, olive oil, Dijon mustard, salt and pepper.
4. Pour the dressing over the salad and toss gently to coat all the ingredients.
5. Let stand in the fridge for at least 30 minutes before serving, to allow the flavours to mingle.
6. Before serving, sprinkle with sesame seeds for an extra touch of crunch.

Present this lentil salad with crunchy vegetables on a large serving platter or in individual bowls. It's ideal as a main course for a nutritious and satisfying lunch.

QUINOA SALAD WITH GRILLED VEGETABLES

SERVINGS

Serves 4

PREPARATION TIME

15 minutes

COOKING TIME

20 minutes

INGREDIENTS

- ✔ 1 cup raw quinoa
- ✔ 2 cups water
- ✔ 2 zucchinis, sliced into rounds
- ✔ 1 eggplant, diced
- ✔ 1 red bell pepper, cut into strips
- ✔ 1 red onion, thinly sliced
- ✔ 2 tablespoons olive oil
- ✔ Salt and pepper to taste
- ✔ ¼ cup chopped fresh parsley
- ✔ Juice of one lemon
- ✔ 2 tablespoons balsamic vinegar
- ✔ 1 avocado, sliced
- ✔ Pumpkin seeds for garnish

INSTRUCTIONS

1. Rinse quinoa under cold running water. In a saucepan, bring 2 cups of water to the boil. Add the quinoa, reduce the heat, cover and simmer for 15 minutes. Remove from the heat, cover and leave to rest for 5 minutes, then remove the seeds with a fork and leave to cool.
2. Preheat your grill or barbecue over medium heat.
3. In a large bowl, toss zucchini slices, diced eggplant, red bell pepper strips, sliced red onion and olive oil. Season with salt and pepper.
4. Grill the vegetables on the preheated grill for approx. 10 – 15 minutes, until tender and charred.
5. In a large bowl, combine the cooked quinoa with the grilled vegetables. Add the chopped fresh parsley, lemon juice and balsamic vinegar. Mix gently.
6. Garnish the salad with avocado slices and sprinkle with pumpkin seeds before serving.

> Present this quinoa salad with grilled vegetables in a serving dish. It can be served warm or cold, and makes a balanced and satisfying lunch.

WHITE BEAN SALAD WITH GRILLED VEGETABLES

SERVINGS

Serves 4

PREPARATION TIME

15 minutes

COOKING TIME

20 minutes

INGREDIENTS

- 2 cans cooked white beans, rinsed and drained
- 2 zucchini, sliced into rounds
- 1 yellow bell pepper, diced
- 1 red onion, thinly sliced
- 2 tablespoons olive oil
- Salt and pepper to taste
- 2 tablespoons balsamic vinegar
- 1 tablespoon honey or agave syrup (low GI: moderate)
- 1 clove garlic, chopped
- ¼ cup chopped fresh parsley
- Fresh basil leaves for garnish

INSTRUCTIONS

1. Preheat your grill or barbecue to medium.
2. In a large bowl, toss zucchini slices, diced yellow bell pepper, minced red onion and olive oil. Season with salt and pepper.
3. Grill the vegetables on the preheated grill for approx. 10 – 15 minutes, until tender and lightly browned. Remove from grill and allow to cool.
4. Mix the cooked white beans with the grilled vegetables in a bowl.
5. In a small bowl, prepare the vinaigrette by mixing the balsamic vinegar, honey or agave syrup, minced garlic, salt and pepper.
6. Pour the dressing over the salad and toss gently to coat all the ingredients.
7. Garnish with chopped fresh parsley and basil leaves before serving.

Serve this white bean and roasted vegetable salad in a large serving dish. It's perfect as a main course for a healthy, balanced lunch.

QUINOA SALAD WITH CRUNCHY VEGETABLES

SERVINGS

Serves 4

PREPARATION TIME

15 minutes

INGREDIENTS

- 1 cup raw quinoa
- 2 cups water
- 1 cucumber, diced
- 2 tomatoes, diced
- 1 red bell pepper, diced
- 1 red onion, thinly sliced
- ¼ cup chopped fresh parsley
- ¼ cup fresh lemon juice
- 3 tablespoons olive oil
- Salt and pepper to taste
- Sunflower seeds for garnish

INSTRUCTIONS

1. Rinse quinoa under cold running water. In a saucepan, bring 2 cups of water to the boil. Add the quinoa, reduce the heat, cover and simmer for 15 minutes. Remove from the heat, cover and leave to rest for 5 minutes, then remove the seeds with a fork and leave to cool.
2. In a large bowl, combine the cooked quinoa, cucumber, tomatoes, red bell pepper, red onion and parsley.
3. In a small bowl, prepare the vinaigrette by mixing the lemon juice with the olive oil. Season with salt and pepper.
4. Pour the dressing over the salad and toss gently to coat all the ingredients.
5. Let the salad rest in the refrigerator for about 30 minutes before serving, to allow the flavors to mingle.
6. Before serving, garnish with sunflower seeds for a crunchy touch.

Serve this quinoa salad with crunchy vegetables in bowls or individual plates. It makes a light, balanced lunch, ideal for a low-glycemic diet.

BROWN RICE SALAD WITH SUMMER VEGETABLES

SERVINGS

Serves 4

PREPARATION TIME

15 minutes

INGREDIENTS

- 1 cup cooked brown rice
- 1 zucchini, diced
- 1 red bell pepper, diced
- 1 yellow bell pepper, diced
- 1 red onion, thinly sliced
- 1 cup cherry tomatoes, halved
- ¼ cup chopped fresh basil
- 3 tablespoons olive oil
- 2 tablespoons balsamic vinegar
- Salt and pepper to taste
- Crumbled goat's cheese for garnish (optional, low GI)

INSTRUCTIONS

1. Heat 1 tablespoon of olive oil in a large frying pan over medium heat. Add the diced zucchini, diced red bell pepper, diced yellow bell pepper and sliced red onion. Sauté for 5 – 7 minutes, until the vegetables are tender-crisp. Remove from heat and allow to cool.
2. In a large bowl, mix the cooked brown rice with the sautéed vegetables, cherry tomatoes and chopped fresh basil.
3. In a small bowl, prepare the vinaigrette by mixing 2 tablespoons of olive oil with the balsamic vinegar. Season with salt and pepper.
4. Pour the dressing over the salad and toss gently to coat all the ingredients.
5. If desired, garnish the salad with crumbled goat's cheese before serving.

> Serve this summer vegetable brown rice salad on individual plates or in a large serving dish. It makes a light, balanced meal for a low-glycemic lunch, perfect for hot days.

SATIATING BREAKFASTS

Balanced sandwiches and wraps

GRILLED VEGETABLE AND HUMMUS SANDWICH

SERVINGS

For 2 sandwiches

PREPARATION TIME

15 minutes

INGREDIENTS

- 4 slices wholemeal bread
- 1 zucchini, cut into thin strips
- 1 red bell pepper, cut into strips
- 1 red onion, sliced into rings
- ½ cup hummus
- 2 tablespoons olive oil
- Salt and pepper to taste
- Lettuce leaves or fresh spinach

INSTRUCTIONS

1. Preheat a frying pan over medium heat. Add 1 tablespoon of olive oil and sauté the zucchini strips, red bell pepper strips and red onion rings for about 5 – 7 minutes, until tender and lightly browned. Season with salt and pepper. Remove from heat and set aside.
2. Spread the hummus on two slices of wholemeal bread.
3. On the other two slices of bread, arrange the fresh lettuce or spinach leaves.
4. Spread the grilled vegetables evenly over the hummus-filled bread slices.
5. Close the sandwiches with the slices of bread topped with lettuce or spinach to form two sandwiches.
6. Cut sandwiches in half if desired and serve.

> Arrange the sandwiches on a plate and serve with crudités or a green salad for a complete, balanced meal. These sandwiches can also be wrapped in parchment paper or aluminum foil for easy transport on the move or for lunches out and about.

GRILLED VEGETABLE AND MARINATED TOFU SANDWICH

SERVINGS

For 2 sandwiches

PREPARATION TIME

20 minutes

COOKING TIME

10 minutes

INGREDIENTS

- 4 slices low GI wholemeal bread
- 200 g firm tofu, sliced
- 1 zucchini, cut into thin strips
- 1 red bell pepper, cut into strips
- 1 red onion, sliced into rings
- 2 tablespoons olive oil
- 2 tablespoons soy sauce (low sugar content)
- 2 tablespoons balsamic vinegar
- A few leaves of arugula or lettuce
- Salt and pepper to taste

INSTRUCTIONS

1. In a bowl, combine the olive oil, soy sauce and balsamic vinegar. Marinate the tofu slices in this mixture for 10 minutes.
2. Heat a grill or frying pan over medium heat. Grill the marinated tofu slices for 3 – 4 minutes on each side, until golden-brown. Remove from the pan and set aside.
3. Use the same pan or grill to grill the zucchini strips, bell pepper strips and onion rings with a little olive oil, until tender and lightly browned. Season with salt and pepper.
4. Arrange the slices of grilled tofu on two slices of bread.
5. Add the grilled vegetables on top of the tofu.
6. Garnish with a few leaves of arugula or lettuce.
7. Cover with the remaining slices of bread to form the sandwiches.

> Serve these sandwiches with lemon wedges or a fresh salad for a balanced, filling meal.

LEGUME AND GUACAMOLE SANDWICH

SERVINGS

For 2 sandwiches

PREPARATION TIME

15 minutes

INGREDIENTS

- 4 slices low GI wholemeal bread
- 1 cup cooked black beans
- 1 small tomato, sliced
- ½ red onion, thinly sliced
- 1 ripe avocado
- Juice of ½ lemon
- A few fresh coriander leaves
- 1 pinch chili flakes (optional, low GI)
- Salt and pepper to taste

INSTRUCTIONS

1. Mash the black beans in a bowl with a fork. Season to taste with salt and pepper.
2. In another bowl, mash the avocado with the lemon juice to prepare the guacamole. Add the chopped coriander leaves, chili flakes (if desired), salt and pepper. Mix well.
3. Generously spread two slices of bread with the crushed black bean mixture.
4. Spread tomato and red onion slices over the bean mixture.
5. Spread the guacamole on the other two slices of bread and place them gently on top of the slices with the vegetables.
6. Cut sandwiches diagonally if desired.

Serve these sandwiches with a few fresh raw vegetables, such as carrot sticks or cucumber slices. You can also present them on a plate with a touch of fresh coriander for a beautiful presentation.

PROTEIN WRAP WITH BLACK BEANS AND AVOCADO

SERVINGS

For 2 wraps

PREPARATION TIME

15 minutes

INGREDIENTS

- 4 low-GI whole-wheat tortillas
- 1 ripe avocado
- 1 can black beans, cooked and drained
- 1 red bell pepper, cut into thin strips
- 1 small red onion, thinly sliced
- ½ cup sweet corn kernels
- 1 tomato, diced
- 1 cup mixed lettuce or baby greens
- Juice of 1 lime
- 2 tablespoons chopped fresh coriander
- Salt and black pepper

INSTRUCTIONS

1. In a bowl, mash the avocado with the lime juice, coriander, salt and pepper to make an avocado purée.
2. Heat tortillas according to package instructions.
3. Spread the avocado purée evenly over each tortilla.
4. Spread the drained black beans over the avocado purée.
5. Add the peppers, onion, corn, diced tomato and lettuce leaves to the black bean layer.
6. Season to taste with salt and pepper.
7. Roll tortillas tightly to form wraps. Cut in half if desired.

> Arrange the wraps on a plate, cut side up, to showcase the vibrant colors of the vegetables inside. Serve with lime wedges for an extra touch of freshness. Serve with a crisp green salad for a balanced, filling lunch.

ROASTED VEGETABLE AND GOAT CHEESE SANDWICH

SERVINGS

For 2 sandwiches

PREPARATION TIME

20 minutes

INGREDIENTS

- 4 slices wholemeal or cereal bread
- 1 eggplant, sliced into rounds
- 1 red bell pepper, cut into strips
- 1 zucchini, cut into rings
- 1 red onion, cut into rings
- 100 g fresh goat's cheese
- 2 tablespoons olive oil
- Salt and pepper to taste
- Arugula or lettuce leaves

INSTRUCTIONS

1. Preheat oven to 200°C. Arrange the eggplant slices, bell pepper strips, zucchini slices and onion rings on a baking sheet. Drizzle with olive oil and season with salt and pepper. Roast in the oven for 15 – 20 minutes, until the vegetables are tender and lightly browned. Remove from oven and allow to cool slightly.
2. Spread the fresh goat's cheese on two slices of bread.
3. Arrange the arugula or lettuce leaves on the other two slices of bread.
4. Divide the roasted vegetables between the slices of bread topped with goat's cheese.
5. Close the sandwiches with the slices of bread topped with arugula or lettuce to form two sandwiches.

> Serve these diagonally-sliced roasted vegetable and goat cheese sandwiches on a cutting board or plate. Serve with vegetable sticks or a green salad for a delicious, low-glycemic meal.

MEDITERRANEAN SANDWICH WITH GRILLED VEGETABLES

SERVINGS

For 2 sandwiches

PREPARATION TIME

20 minutes

INGREDIENTS

- 4 slices wholemeal or cereal bread
- 1 eggplant, sliced into rounds
- 1 yellow bell pepper, cut into strips
- 1 zucchini, cut into rings
- 1 red onion, cut into rings
- 2 tablespoons olive oil
- Salt and pepper to taste
- 4 tablespoons olive tapenade
- Fresh basil leaves

INSTRUCTIONS

1. Preheat a grill pan or grill to medium-high heat. Brush eggplant slices, bell pepper strips, zucchini slices and onion rings with olive oil. Season with salt and pepper.
2. Grill the vegetables for approx. 5 – 7 minutes on each side, until tender and lightly browned. Remove from heat and allow to cool slightly.
3. Spread the olive tapenade generously on two slices of bread.
4. Arrange the grilled vegetables on the other two slices of bread.
5. Add a few fresh basil leaves to the vegetables.
6. Close the sandwiches to form two portions.

> Serve these Mediterranean sandwiches with grilled vegetables cut diagonally and arranged on a plate. Serve with a green salad or tomato wedges for an extra touch of freshness.

WRAP WITH SAUTÉED MUSHROOMS AND CHICKPEA HUMMUS

SERVINGS

For 2 wraps

PREPARATION TIME

15 minutes

COOKING TIME

Mushroom cooking time: 10 minutes

INGREDIENTS

- 4 low-GI whole-wheat tortillas
- 250 g sliced mushrooms
- 2 tablespoons olive oil
- 2 cloves garlic, minced
- 1 teaspoon fresh thyme
- Salt and black pepper

For the hummus

- 1 can cooked and drained chickpeas
- 2 tablespoons tahini
- Juice of 1 lemon
- 2 tablespoons olive oil
- Salt and black pepper
- Lettuce leaves for garnish

INSTRUCTIONS

1. Heat a tablespoon of olive oil in a frying pan over medium heat. Add the sliced mushrooms and sauté for about 5 minutes, until they start to brown. Add the garlic, thyme, salt and pepper. Continue cooking for 3 – 4 minutes until the mushrooms are tender. Set aside.
2. Prepare the hummus: in a blender, combine the drained chickpeas, tahini, lemon juice, olive oil, salt and pepper. Blend until smooth and creamy.
3. Lightly heat tortillas according to package instructions.
4. Spread a generous layer of hummus on each tortilla.
5. Sprinkle the sautéed mushrooms over the hummus.
6. Add lettuce leaves for garnish, if desired.
7. Roll tortillas tightly to form wraps.

> Arrange the wraps on a serving plate and cut on the bias for a neat presentation. Serve with fresh vegetable sticks (such as carrots or cucumbers) and a small portion of extra hummus for dipping. This creates a tasty and satisfying lunch.

SATIATING BREAKFASTS

Takeaway lunch options

VEGETABLE QUINOA SALAD FOR PACKED LUNCHES

SERVINGS

For 2 servings

PREPARATION TIME

15 minutes

INGREDIENTS

- 1 cup raw quinoa
- 2 cups water
- ½ cucumber, diced
- 1 tomato, diced
- ½ red bell pepper, diced
- ¼ cup chopped fresh coriander
- Juice of ½ lemon
- 2 tablespoons olive oil
- Salt and pepper to taste
- Sunflower seeds for garnish

INSTRUCTIONS

1. Rinse quinoa under cold running water. In a saucepan, bring 2 cups of water to the boil. Add the quinoa, reduce the heat, cover and simmer for 15 minutes. Remove from the heat, cover and leave to rest for 5 minutes, then remove the seeds with a fork and leave to cool.
2. In a large bowl, combine the cooked quinoa, cucumber, tomato, red bell pepper and chopped coriander.
3. Prepare the vinaigrette by mixing the lemon juice with the olive oil. Season with salt and pepper.
4. Pour the dressing over the salad and toss gently to coat all the ingredients.
5. Divide the vegetable quinoa salad between airtight containers for transport.
6. Just before serving, sprinkle with sunflower seeds for a crunchy touch.

> Arrange quinoa salad in individual airtight containers for a convenient packed lunch. Serve with lemon wedges or a light vinaigrette for those who prefer extra seasoning.

CRISP VEGETABLE WRAP WITH CHICKPEA SPREAD

SERVINGS

For 2 wraps

PREPARATION TIME

15 minutes

INGREDIENTS

- 2 whole-wheat or seed tortillas
- 1 cup cooked chickpeas
- 2 tablespoons tahini (sesame paste, low GI)
- Juice of half a lemon
- 1 small carrot, cut into thin strips
- 1 cucumber, cut into strips
- ½ red bell pepper, cut into strips
- Lettuce leaves or fresh spinach
- 2 tablespoons olive oil
- Salt and pepper to taste

INSTRUCTIONS

1. In a blender, blend the cooked chickpeas, tahini, lemon juice, 1 tablespoon olive oil, salt and pepper until smooth.
2. Spread the chickpea spread on the tortillas.
3. Arrange the lettuce or spinach leaves on top.
4. Divide the carrot, cucumber and bell pepper strips among the lettuce or spinach leaves.
5. Fold in the sides of the tortillas and roll up tightly to form two wraps.
6. Cut the wraps in half for convenient presentation and pack in aluminum foil or airtight containers for lunch.

Wrap wraps individually in aluminum foil or place in airtight containers for easy transport. Serve with extra vegetable sticks or lemon wedges for a variety of flavors and textures at lunchtime.

LENTIL AND VEGETABLE SALAD FOR A NOMADIC LUNCH

SERVINGS

For 2 servings

PREPARATION TIME

15 minutes

INGREDIENTS

- 1 cup cooked lentils
- 1 tomato, diced
- ½ cucumber, diced
- 1 red bell pepper, diced
- 1 carrot, grated
- 2 tablespoons balsamic vinegar
- 2 tablespoons olive oil
- Salt and pepper to taste
- Fresh parsley leaves, chopped

INSTRUCTIONS

1. In a large bowl, combine the cooked lentils, diced tomato, cucumber, bell pepper and grated carrot.
2. Prepare the vinaigrette by mixing the balsamic vinegar with the olive oil. Season with salt and pepper.
3. Pour the vinaigrette over the lentil salad and toss gently to coat all the vegetables.
4. Sprinkle with chopped parsley leaves for extra freshness.

Divide lentil and vegetable salad into individual airtight containers for a convenient on-the-go lunch. This salad can be served cold and is easy to transport, making it an ideal option for a healthy, balanced lunch on the go.

WRAP WITH GRILLED VEGETABLES AND FETA CHEESE

SERVINGS

For 2 wraps

PREPARATION TIME

20 minutes

INGREDIENTS

- ✔ 2 whole-wheat or seed tortillas
- ✔ 1 zucchini, cut into strips
- ✔ 1 red bell pepper, cut into strips
- ✔ 1 red onion, thinly sliced
- ✔ 100 g feta cheese, crumbled
- ✔ 2 tablespoons olive oil
- ✔ Salt and pepper to taste
- ✔ Lettuce leaves or arugula

INSTRUCTIONS

1. Preheat a frying pan or grill over medium-high heat. Add 1 tablespoon of olive oil and sauté the zucchini strips, red bell pepper and sliced red onion for 5 to 7 minutes, until tender. Season with salt and pepper. Set aside.
2. Spread lettuce or arugula leaves on each tortilla.
3. Divide the grilled vegetables among the lettuce or arugula leaves.
4. Sprinkle the crumbled feta cheese over the vegetables.
5. Fold in the sides of the tortillas and roll up tightly to form two wraps.
6. Cut the wraps in half for easy transport and wrap in aluminum foil or place in airtight containers to take away.

> Wrap each wrap half individually in aluminum foil for convenient portability. Serve with lemon wedges or vegetable sticks to complete this takeaway lunch.

QUINOA SALAD WITH VEGETABLES AND AVOCADO

SERVINGS

For 2 servings

PREPARATION TIME

20 minutes

INGREDIENTS

- 1 cup raw quinoa
- 2 cups water
- 1 ripe avocado, diced
- 1 tomato, diced
- ½ cucumber, diced
- ¼ cup chopped fresh parsley
- Juice of 1 lemon
- 2 tablespoons olive oil
- Salt and pepper to taste
- Optional: chia seeds for garnish

INSTRUCTIONS

1. Rinse quinoa under cold running water. In a saucepan, bring 2 cups of water to the boil. Add the quinoa, reduce the heat, cover and simmer for 15 minutes. Remove from the heat, cover and leave to rest for 5 minutes, then remove the seeds with a fork and leave to cool.
2. In a large bowl, combine the cooked quinoa, diced avocado, tomato and cucumber, and chopped parsley.
3. Prepare the vinaigrette by mixing the lemon juice with the olive oil. Season with salt and pepper.
4. Pour the dressing over the quinoa salad and toss gently to coat all the ingredients.
5. Sprinkle with chia seeds for a touch of crunch and extra nutrients.

> Divide quinoa salad between airtight containers for a packed lunch. It's easy to transport and a delicious, nutritious option. Serve with a slice of lemon for those who like a little more acidity.

SATIATING BREAKFASTS

Vegetarian hot dishes for lunch

PAN-FRIED VEGETABLES WITH QUINOA

SERVINGS

For 2 servings

PREPARATION TIME

15 minutes

COOKING TIME

20 minutes

INGREDIENTS

- 1 cup raw quinoa
- 2 cups water
- 1 zucchini, diced
- 1 red bell pepper, diced
- 1 onion, chopped
- 2 garlic cloves, chopped
- 1 tablespoon olive oil
- 1 teaspoon cumin powder
- 1 teaspoon paprika
- Salt and pepper to taste
- Chopped fresh coriander leaves for garnish

INSTRUCTIONS

1. Rinse quinoa under cold running water. In a saucepan, bring 2 cups of water to the boil. Add the quinoa, reduce the heat, cover and simmer for 15 minutes. Remove from the heat, cover and leave to rest for 5 minutes, then remove the seeds with a fork and set aside.
2. Heat the olive oil in a large frying pan over medium heat. Add the chopped onion and sauté for 2 – 3 minutes until translucent.
3. Add the chopped garlic, red bell pepper and zucchini. Sauté for about 5 minutes until the vegetables are slightly tender.
4. Stir in cumin powder, paprika, salt and pepper. Mix well to coat all the vegetables with the spices.
5. Add the cooked quinoa to the pan with the vegetables. Mix gently to combine all the ingredients and reheat for 2 – 3 minutes.
6. Serve the pan-fried vegetables with quinoa on individual plates and garnish with fresh coriander.

> Serve the pan-fried vegetables with quinoa in bowls or soup plates. You can accompany this dish with a slice of lemon or a light yogurt-based sauce for an extra touch of freshness and flavor.

PASTA WITH GRILLED VEGETABLES AND HOMEMADE TOMATO SAUCE

SERVINGS

Serves 4

PREPARATION TIME

15 minutes

COOKING TIME

25 minutes

INGREDIENTS

- 300 g wholegrain pasta
- 2 tablespoons olive oil
- 1 onion, chopped
- 2 garlic cloves, minced
- 2 peppers (red and yellow), cut into strips
- 1 zucchini, sliced into rings
- 400 g canned crushed tomatoes
- 1 teaspoon dried oregano
- Salt and pepper to taste
- A few fresh basil leaves for garnish

INSTRUCTIONS

1. Cook pasta according to package instructions in boiling salted water. Drain and set aside.
2. Heat the olive oil in a large frying pan over medium heat. Add the onion and garlic and sauté until translucent.
3. Add the peppers and zucchini to the pan. Sauté for about 5 – 7 minutes, until tender-crisp.
4. Stir in the crushed tomatoes and oregano. Season with salt and pepper. Simmer for 10 minutes over low heat.
5. Add the cooked pasta to the pan with the vegetables and sauce. Toss gently to coat the pasta.
6. Garnish with fresh basil leaves before serving.

> Serve this pasta with grilled vegetables and homemade tomato sauce in soup plates, garnished with fresh basil leaves. Serve with a green salad for a balanced meal.

VEGETABLE AND TOFU CURRY

SERVINGS

For 2 servings

PREPARATION TIME

15 minutes

COOKING TIME

20 minutes

INGREDIENTS

- ✔ 200 g firm tofu, cubed
- ✔ 1 tablespoon coconut oil
- ✔ 1 onion, chopped
- ✔ 2 garlic cloves, chopped
- ✔ 1 teaspoon fresh ginger, grated
- ✔ 1 red bell pepper, cut into strips
- ✔ 1 zucchini, diced
- ✔ 1 can (400 ml) coconut milk
- ✔ 2 tablespoons curry paste
- ✔ Salt and pepper to taste
- ✔ Chopped fresh coriander leaves for garnish

INSTRUCTIONS

1. Heat the coconut oil in a frying pan or wok over medium heat. Add the tofu cubes and brown on all sides for around 5 minutes. Remove the tofu from the pan and set aside.
2. In the same pan, add the chopped onion, minced garlic and grated ginger. Fry for 2 – 3 minutes until lightly browned.
3. Add the red bell pepper strips and diced zucchini. Sauté for 5 minutes until vegetables are slightly tender.
4. Stir the curry paste into the vegetables and mix well to coat.
5. Pour the coconut milk into the pan and stir to combine all the ingredients. Simmer for 5 minutes.
6. Add the browned tofu cubes to the pan with the vegetables and simmer for a further 5 minutes.
7. Season to taste with salt and pepper.

> This vegetable and tofu curry is a delicious, balanced combination with a low glycemic index. The rich flavors and protein of tofu make it a satisfying hot dish for lunch.

CHILI VÉGÉTARIEN AUX HARICOTS

SERVINGS

Serves 4

PREPARATION TIME

15 minutes

COOKING TIME

30 minutes

INGREDIENTS

- 2 tablespoons olive oil
- 1 onion, chopped
- 2 garlic cloves, chopped
- 1 red bell pepper, diced
- 1 green bell pepper, diced
- 1 carrot, diced
- 1 - 400 g tin cooked kidney beans, rinsed and drained
- 1 can (400 g) crushed tomatoes
- 1 tablespoon tomato purée
- 1 teaspoon cumin powder
- 1 teaspoon paprika
- ½ teaspoon chili powder (adjust according to spiciness preference)
- Salt and pepper to taste
- Chopped fresh coriander leaves for garnish

INSTRUCTIONS

1. Heat the olive oil in a large saucepan over medium heat. Add the onion and sauté for 2 – 3 minutes, until translucent.
2. Add the chopped garlic, diced red and green peppers and diced carrot. Sauté for about 5 minutes, until the vegetables begin to soften.
3. Add drained kidney beans, crushed tomatoes, tomato paste, cumin powder, paprika, chili powder, salt and pepper. Mix all ingredients well.
4. Simmer over low heat for about 20 minutes, stirring occasionally, to allow the flavors to blend and the vegetables to cook through.
5. Adjust seasoning if necessary.

> Serve the Vegetarian Bean Chili in individual bowls, sprinkled with chopped fresh coriander. Serve with lime wedges and a few slices of avocado for a touch of freshness and creaminess.

RATATOUILLE PROVENÇALE

SERVINGS

Serves 4

PREPARATION TIME

15 minutes

COOKING TIME

30 minutes

INGREDIENTS

- 2 tablespoons olive oil
- 1 onion, chopped
- 2 garlic cloves, minced
- 1 eggplant, diced
- 1 zucchini, diced
- 2 peppers (red and green), diced
- 4 tomatoes, diced
- 2 tablespoons tomato paste
- 1 teaspoon herbes de Provence
- Salt and pepper to taste
- A few fresh basil leaves for garnish

INSTRUCTIONS

1. Heat the olive oil in a large saucepan over medium heat. Add the onion and garlic and sauté until translucent.
2. Add the eggplant, zucchini and peppers to the pan. Sauté for about 10 minutes, until the vegetables begin to soften.
3. Add the diced tomatoes, tomato paste, herbes de Provence, salt and pepper. Mix well.
4. Simmer over low heat for 20 minutes, stirring occasionally, until vegetables are tender and flavors blend.
5. Garnish with fresh basil leaves before serving.

> Serve this warm ratatouille provençale in soup plates, accompanied by wholemeal bread or quinoa for a tasty, vegetable-rich, low-glycemic breakfast.

TASTY DINNERS

Legume and whole-grain dishes

QUINOA AND BLACK BEAN BOWL

SERVINGS

For 2 servings

PREPARATION TIME

15 minutes

COOKING TIME

20 minutes

INGREDIENTS

- ✔ 1 cup raw quinoa
- ✔ 2 cups water
- ✔ 1 can (400 g) cooked black beans, rinsed and drained
- ✔ 1 avocado, sliced
- ✔ 1 tomato, diced
- ✔ ½ red onion, thinly sliced
- ✔ Juice of 1 lime
- ✔ 2 tablespoons olive oil
- ✔ Salt and pepper to taste
- ✔ Chopped fresh coriander leaves for garnish

INSTRUCTIONS

1. Rinse quinoa under cold running water. In a saucepan, bring 2 cups of water to the boil. Add the quinoa, reduce the heat, cover and simmer for 15 minutes. Remove from the heat, cover and leave to rest for 5 minutes, then remove the seeds with a fork and set aside.
2. In a bowl, combine the cooked black beans, diced tomato, finely sliced red onion, lime juice and olive oil. Season with salt and pepper.
3. Divide the cooked quinoa between individual bowls.
4. Arrange the black bean mixture on top of the quinoa.
5. Add avocado slices on top.
6. Garnish with chopped fresh coriander leaves.

> Serve this quinoa and black bean bowl in deep bowls for an attractive presentation. You can also add a dollop of plain Greek yoghurt on top for a creamy touch, or accompany the dish with lime wedges for added freshness.

SALADE DE LENTILLES ET BOULGOUR

SERVINGS

For 2 servings

PREPARATION TIME

15 minutes

INGREDIENTS

- ½ cup cooked green lentils
- ½ cup cooked bulgur
- 1 cucumber, diced
- 1 red bell pepper, diced
- 2 tomatoes, diced
- 1 red onion, thinly sliced
- Juice of 1 lemon
- 2 tablespoons olive oil
- 1 teaspoon cumin powder
- Salt and pepper to taste
- Chopped fresh mint leaves for garnish

INSTRUCTIONS

1. In a large bowl, combine the cooked lentils, cooked bulgur, diced cucumber, red bell pepper, tomato and sliced red onion.
2. Prepare the vinaigrette by mixing the lemon juice with the olive oil and cumin powder. Season with salt and pepper.
3. Pour the dressing over the salad and toss gently to coat all the ingredients.
4. Sprinkle with chopped fresh mint leaves before serving.

Serve this lentil and bulgur salad on individual plates. You can also present it on a large platter so that everyone at the table can help themselves. Serve with a portion of sliced avocado or crumbled feta for added flavor and creaminess.

PAN-FRIED CHICKPEAS AND QUINOA

SERVINGS

For 2 servings

PREPARATION TIME

15 minutes

COOKING TIME

20 minutes

INGREDIENTS

- 1 cup raw quinoa
- 2 cups water
- 1 can (400 g) cooked chickpeas, rinsed and drained
- 1 yellow bell pepper, diced
- 1 zucchini, diced
- 1 onion, finely chopped
- 2 garlic cloves, chopped
- 2 tablespoons olive oil
- 1 teaspoon paprika
- 1 teaspoon cumin powder
- Salt and pepper to taste
- Fresh parsley leaves, chopped, for garnish

INSTRUCTIONS

1. Rinse quinoa under cold running water. In a saucepan, bring 2 cups of water to the boil. Add the quinoa, reduce the heat, cover and simmer for 15 minutes. Remove from the heat, cover and leave to rest for 5 minutes, then remove the seeds with a fork and set aside.

2. Heat the olive oil in a large frying pan over medium heat. Add the finely chopped onion and sauté for 2 – 3 minutes until translucent.

3. Add the chopped garlic, diced yellow bell pepper and diced zucchini. Sauté for 5 minutes until the vegetables are slightly tender.

4. Add the drained chickpeas to the pan with the vegetables. Add paprika, cumin, salt and pepper. Mix well and cook for 5 minutes.

5. Add the cooked quinoa to the pan with the vegetable and chickpea mixture. Mix gently to combine all the ingredients and reheat for 2 – 3 minutes.

6. Serve the chickpea and quinoa pan-fry on individual plates. Garnish with chopped fresh parsley leaves before serving.

Serve this chickpea and quinoa pan-fried dish in bowls or soup plates. Serve with a yoghurt and lemon sauce for an added touch of freshness and flavor.

LENTIL AND VEGETABLE CURRY

SERVINGS

Serves 4

PREPARATION TIME

15 minutes

COOKING TIME

25 minutes

INGREDIENTS

- 1 cup coral lentils
- 2 tablespoons olive oil
- 1 onion, chopped
- 2 cloves garlic, minced
- 1 carrot, diced
- 1 zucchini, diced
- 1 red bell pepper, diced
- 1 can 400 ml coconut milk
- 2 tablespoons curry paste
- 1 teaspoon turmeric powder
- Salt and pepper to taste
- Chopped fresh coriander leaves for garnish

INSTRUCTIONS

1. Rinse the coral lentils in cold water. Heat the olive oil in a saucepan over medium heat. Add the chopped onion and minced garlic and sauté for 2 – 3 minutes, until soft.
2. Add the diced carrot, zucchini and red bell pepper. Sauté for about 5 minutes, until the vegetables begin to soften.
3. Add the coral lentils and mix well with the vegetables.
4. Add the curry paste and turmeric powder and toss to coat the vegetables and lentils.
5. Pour the coconut milk into the pan. Season to taste with salt and pepper.
6. Simmer over a low heat for 15 minutes, until the lentils and vegetables are tender.

> Serve lentil curry with vegetables in individual bowls, sprinkled with chopped fresh coriander leaves. Serve with basmati rice or naan bread for a complete and balanced meal.

FRIED QUINOA WITH VEGETABLES

SERVINGS

Serves 4

PREPARATION TIME

15 minutes

COOKING TIME

20 minutes

> Serve the vegetable quinoa pan on individual plates. Garnish with chopped fresh basil leaves before serving.

INGREDIENTS

- 1 cup raw quinoa
- 2 cups water
- 2 tablespoons olive oil
- 1 onion, finely chopped
- 2 cloves garlic, chopped
- 1 red bell pepper, diced
- 1 zucchini, diced
- 1 eggplant, diced
- 1 tin (400 g) crushed tomatoes
- 1 teaspoon paprika
- 1 teaspoon dried oregano
- Salt and pepper to taste
- Chopped fresh basil leaves for garnish

INSTRUCTIONS

1. Rinse quinoa under cold running water. In a saucepan, bring 2 cups of water to the boil. Add the quinoa, reduce the heat, cover and simmer for 15 minutes. Remove from the heat, cover and leave to rest for 5 minutes, then remove the seeds with a fork and set aside.

2. Heat the olive oil in a large frying pan over medium heat. Add the finely sliced onion and minced garlic, and sauté for 2 – 3 minutes until soft.

3. Add the diced red bell pepper, zucchini and eggplant to the pan. Sauté for about 5 minutes until the vegetables begin to soften.

4. Stir the crushed tomatoes into the pan with the vegetables. Add paprika, dried oregano, salt and pepper. Simmer for 5 – 7 minutes.

5. Add the cooked quinoa to the pan with the vegetable mixture. Stir gently to combine all the ingredients and reheat for 2 – 3 minutes.

ROASTED CHICKPEAS WITH VEGETABLES

SERVINGS

Serves 4

PREPARATION TIME

15 minutes

COOKING TIME

25 minutes

INGREDIENTS

- 2 cans (400 g each) cooked chickpeas, rinsed and drained
- 3 tablespoons olive oil
- 1 teaspoon paprika
- 1 teaspoon cumin powder
- 1 zucchini, diced
- 1 red bell pepper, diced
- 1 red onion, diced
- 2 garlic cloves, chopped
- Salt and pepper to taste
- Fresh parsley leaves, chopped, for garnish

INSTRUCTIONS

1. Preheat oven to 200°C (gas mark 6-7).
2. In a large bowl, toss drained chickpeas with 2 tablespoons olive oil, paprika, cumin, salt and pepper.
3. Arrange the chickpeas on a baking tray lined with parchment paper and roast in the oven for 20 minutes, until crisp.
4. Meanwhile, heat 1 tablespoon of olive oil in a frying pan over medium heat. Add the chopped onion, chopped garlic, zucchini and red bell pepper. Sauté for 5 – 7 minutes, until vegetables are tender.
5. Add the roasted chickpeas to the pan with the sautéed vegetables. Stir gently to combine all the ingredients and reheat for 2 – 3 minutes.
6. Serve the roasted chickpeas with vegetables on plates. Garnish with chopped fresh parsley leaves before serving.

> This dish can be accompanied by a portion of basmati rice or quinoa for a complete meal. You can also add a touch of plain yoghurt on top for extra creaminess and freshness.

QUINOA GALETTES WITH BLACK BEANS

SERVINGS

Serves 4

PREPARATION TIME

15 minutes

COOKING TIME

20 minutes

INGREDIENTS

- 1 cup cooked quinoa (low GI: 53)
- 1 can cooked black beans (low GI: 20)
- 1 red onion, finely chopped
- 2 cloves garlic, minced
- 2 tablespoons chickpea flour (low GI: 10)
- 1 teaspoon cumin powder
- 1 teaspoon paprika
- Salt and pepper to taste
- Olive oil for cooking

INSTRUCTIONS

1. In a large bowl, mash the black beans with a fork until coarsely smooth.
2. Add the cooked quinoa, chopped onion, minced garlic, chickpea flour, cumin powder, paprika, salt and pepper. Mix well to form a homogeneous paste.
3. Divide the dough into equal portions and shape into patties with your hands.
4. Heat a little olive oil in a frying pan over medium heat. Place the quinoa patties in the hot pan.
5. Cook for about 4 – 5 minutes on each side, until golden and crisp.
6. Once cooked, remove the patties from the pan and place on kitchen paper to remove excess oil.

Arrange the black bean quinoa patties on a serving platter. Serve with a lemon coriander sauce or a Greek yoghurt and cucumber sauce for a fresh contrast. Serve with a crisp vegetable salad for a balanced and delicious vegetarian meal.

TOFU SAUTÉ WITH VEGETABLES AND SESAME SEEDS

SERVINGS

For 2 servings

PREPARATION TIME

15 minutes

COOKING TIME

15 minutes

INGREDIENTS

- 200 g firm tofu, cubed
- 2 tablespoons low-sodium soy sauce
- 1 tablespoon sesame oil
- 1 tablespoon olive oil
- 1 red bell pepper, cut into strips
- 1 carrot, julienned
- 1 zucchini, sliced into rings
- 2 garlic cloves, chopped
- 1 teaspoon sesame seeds
- Salt and pepper to taste
- Chopped fresh coriander for garnish

INSTRUCTIONS

1. In a bowl, marinate the tofu cubes in the soy sauce for 10 minutes.
2. In a frying pan or wok, heat the olive oil and sesame oil over medium heat. Add the chopped garlic and sauté for 1 minute.
3. Add the marinated tofu to the pan and stir-fry for 5 – 6 minutes, until golden.
4. Add the bell pepper strips, carrot julienne and zucchini slices to the pan. Sauté for about 5 minutes, until the vegetables are tender-crisp.
5. Season to taste with salt and pepper. Sprinkle with sesame seeds and toss gently.
6. Serve the tofu sautéed with vegetables on individual plates. Garnish with chopped fresh coriander before serving.

Serve with steamed basmati rice for a balanced, complete meal. You can also add a touch of chilli or sriracha sauce for extra spicy flavour.

TASTY DINNERS

Varieties of vegetable dishes and plant proteins

CHICKPEA AND SWEET POTATO CURRY

SERVINGS

Serves 4

PREPARATION TIME

15 minutes

COOKING TIME

25 minutes

INGREDIENTS

- 2 tablespoons olive oil
- 1 onion, chopped
- 2 garlic cloves, minced
- 2 tablespoons curry paste
- 2 sweet potatoes, peeled and cubed
- 2 cans 400 g cooked chickpeas, rinsed and drained
- 400 ml coconut milk
- 200 ml vegetable stock
- Salt and pepper to taste
- Chopped fresh coriander for garnish

INSTRUCTIONS

1. In a large frying pan or saucepan, heat the olive oil over medium heat. Add the chopped onion and minced garlic. Sauté for 2 – 3 minutes, until tender.
2. Add the curry paste to the pan and stir with the onion and garlic for 1 minute to release the aromas.
3. Add the sweet potato cubes and sauté for 5 minutes.
4. Add the drained chickpeas to the pan. Pour in the coconut milk and vegetable stock. Season to taste with salt and pepper. Simmer for 15 minutes over low heat until the sweet potatoes are tender.
5. Adjust seasoning if necessary. Garnish with chopped fresh coriander before serving.

> Serve the chickpea and sweet potato curry in individual bowls, accompanied by basmati rice or quinoa for a complete meal. You can also add lime wedges for a touch of acidity.

RATATOUILLE WITH WHITE BEANS

SERVINGS

Serves 4

PREPARATION TIME

15 minutes

COOKING TIME

30 minutes

INGREDIENTS

- 2 tablespoons olive oil
- 1 onion, chopped
- 2 garlic cloves, minced
- 1 eggplant, diced
- 1 zucchini, diced
- 1 red bell pepper, diced
- 400 g canned crushed tomatoes
- 400 g cooked white beans, rinsed and drained
- 1 teaspoon herbes de Provence
- Salt and pepper to taste
- Chopped fresh basil leaves for garnish

INSTRUCTIONS

1. Heat the olive oil in a large frying pan or casserole over medium heat. Add the chopped onion and minced garlic. Sauté for 2 – 3 minutes until translucent.
2. Add the diced eggplant, zucchini and red bell pepper to the pan. Sauté for about 5 minutes, until the vegetables begin to soften.
3. Add the canned crushed tomatoes to the pan with the vegetables. Add the drained white beans, herbes de Provence, salt and pepper. Mix gently.
4. Simmer over low heat for 20 – 25 minutes, until all the vegetables are tender and the flavors have combined.
5. Adjust seasoning to taste. Garnish with chopped fresh basil leaves before serving.

Serve ratatouille with white beans in soup plates. Serve with toasted wholemeal bread or quinoa for a balanced meal. This ratatouille can also be delicious served with a vegetable protein such as grilled tofu.

PAN-FRIED VEGETABLES WITH LENTILS

SERVINGS

Serves 4

PREPARATION TIME

15 minutes

COOKING TIME

25 minutes

INGREDIENTS

- 1 cup cooked green lentils
- 2 tablespoons olive oil
- 1 onion, chopped
- 2 cloves garlic, minced
- 1 red bell pepper, diced
- 1 zucchini, diced
- 1 eggplant, diced
- 400 g canned crushed tomatoes
- 1 teaspoon paprika
- 1 teaspoon cumin powder
- Salt and pepper to taste
- Chopped fresh parsley leaves for garnish

INSTRUCTIONS

1. Heat the olive oil in a large frying pan over medium heat. Add the chopped onion and minced garlic. Sauté for 2 – 3 minutes until tender.
2. Add the diced red bell pepper, zucchini and eggplant to the pan. Sauté for about 5 minutes, until the vegetables begin to soften.
3. Add the canned crushed tomatoes to the pan with the vegetables. Add the cooked lentils, paprika, cumin, salt and pepper. Mix well.
4. Simmer over a low heat for 15 – 20 minutes, until all the vegetables are tender and the flavors have blended.
5. Adjust seasoning if necessary. Garnish with chopped fresh parsley leaves before serving.

Serve the pan-fried lentil vegetables in soup plates. Serve with toasted wholemeal bread or basmati rice for a complete, balanced meal.

TOFU AND VEGETABLE CURRY

SERVINGS

Serves 4

PREPARATION TIME

15 minutes

COOKING TIME

25 minutes

INGREDIENTS

- 400 g firm tofu, cubed
- 2 tablespoons coconut oil
- 1 onion, chopped
- 2 cloves garlic, minced
- 1 tbsp. curry paste
- 1 teaspoon turmeric powder
- 1 red bell pepper, cut into strips
- 1 zucchini, sliced into rings
- 200 ml coconut milk
- 1 tablespoon low-sodium soy sauce
- Salt and pepper to taste
- Chopped fresh coriander for garnish

INSTRUCTIONS

1. Heat the coconut oil in a large frying pan over medium heat. Add the chopped onion and minced garlic. Sauté for 2 – 3 minutes until translucent.
2. Add the curry paste and turmeric to the pan. Stir for 1 minute to release the aromas.
3. Add the tofu cubes to the pan and fry for 5 – 6 minutes until lightly browned.
4. Add the red bell pepper strips and zucchini slices to the pan with the tofu. Sauté for 3 – 4 minutes.
5. Pour the coconut milk into the pan, add the soy sauce, salt and pepper. Simmer over low heat for 8 – 10 minutes, until the vegetables are tender.
6. Adjust seasoning if necessary. Garnish with chopped fresh coriander before serving.

> Serve the tofu and vegetable curry in individual bowls, accompanied by basmati rice or quinoa for a complete, balanced meal.

CHICKPEA AND SPINACH CURRY

SERVINGS

Serves 4

PREPARATION TIME

10 minutes

COOKING TIME

20 minutes

INGREDIENTS

- 2 tablespoons olive oil
- 1 onion, chopped
- 2 garlic cloves, minced
- 1 tablespoon curry paste
- 400 g cooked chickpeas, rinsed and drained
- 200 g canned crushed tomatoes
- 200 ml coconut milk
- 200 g fresh spinach
- Salt and pepper to taste
- Chopped fresh coriander for garnish

INSTRUCTIONS

1. Heat the olive oil in a large frying pan over medium heat. Add the chopped onion and minced garlic. Sauté for 2 – 3 minutes until tender.
2. Add the curry paste to the pan. Stir with the onion and garlic for 1 minute to release the aromas.
3. Add the drained chickpeas, canned crushed tomatoes and coconut milk to the pan. Season with salt and pepper. Simmer for 10 minutes over low heat.
4. Add the fresh spinach to the pan and gently toss until slightly wilted, about 3 – 4 minutes.
5. Adjust seasoning if necessary. Garnish with chopped fresh coriander before serving.

> Serve this chickpea and spinach curry in individual bowls with basmati rice or cooked quinoa. You can also accompany this dish with a portion of wholegrain naan for a more complete meal.

TOFU SAUTÉ WITH CRUNCHY VEGETABLES

SERVINGS

Serves 4

PREPARATION TIME

15 minutes

COOKING TIME

15 minutes

INGREDIENTS

- 400 g firm tofu, cubed
- 2 tablespoons olive oil
- 2 cloves garlic, minced
- 1 onion, thinly sliced
- 1 red bell pepper, cut into strips
- 1 green bell pepper, cut into strips
- 1 zucchini, sliced into rings
- 200 g mushrooms, sliced
- 2 tablespoons low-sodium soy sauce
- Salt and pepper to taste
- Sesame seeds for garnish (optional, low GI)
- Chopped fresh coriander for garnish

INSTRUCTIONS

1. In a large frying pan or wok, heat olive oil over medium heat. Add minced onion and minced garlic. Sauté for 2 – 3 minutes until tender.
2. Add the tofu cubes to the pan. Sauté for about 5 minutes until golden on all sides.
3. Add the bell pepper strips, zucchini slices and mushrooms to the pan with the tofu. Sauté for 5 – 7 minutes, until vegetables are tender-crisp.
4. Add the soy sauce to the pan and mix all the ingredients together. Season to taste with salt and pepper.
5. Remove from heat and garnish with sesame seeds (if using) and chopped fresh coriander.

> Serve sautéed tofu with crunchy vegetables in individual bowls. Serve with brown rice or quinoa for a balanced, tasty meal.

RATATOUILLE WITH FRESH HERBS

SERVINGS

Serves 4

PREPARATION TIME

20 minutes

COOKING TIME

30 minutes

INGREDIENTS

- 2 tablespoons olive oil
- 1 onion, chopped
- 2 garlic cloves, minced
- 1 eggplant, diced
- 1 zucchini, diced
- 1 red bell pepper, diced
- 400 g canned crushed tomatoes
- 1 teaspoon herbes de Provence
- 1 bay leaf
- Salt and pepper to taste
- A few fresh basil leaves for garnish

INSTRUCTIONS

1. In a large saucepan or casserole, heat the olive oil over medium heat. Add the chopped onion and minced garlic. Sauté for 2 – 3 minutes, until tender.
2. Add the diced eggplant, zucchini and red bell pepper to the pan. Cook for about 5 minutes, until the vegetables begin to soften.
3. Add the canned crushed tomatoes to the pan with the vegetables. Add the herbes de Provence, bay leaf, salt and pepper. Mix well.
4. Simmer over low heat for about 20 minutes, stirring occasionally, until all the vegetables are tender and the flavors are blended.
5. Remove the bay leaf from the ratatouille. Adjust the seasoning if necessary.
6. Serve the ratatouille in soup plates and garnish with fresh basil leaves before serving.

> Serve this ratatouille with toasted wholemeal bread or quinoa for a balanced, satisfying meal.

TASTY DINNERS

Plant-based alternatives to traditional dishes

VEGETARIAN VEGETABLE LASAGNE

SERVINGS

Serves 4

PREPARATION TIME

20 minutes

COOKING TIME

40 minutes

INGREDIENTS

- 1 zucchini, thinly sliced
- 1 eggplant, thinly sliced
- 200 g mushrooms, sliced
- 1 tablespoon olive oil
- 400 g canned crushed tomatoes
- 2 tablespoons tomato paste
- 1 clove garlic, minced
- 1 teaspoon herbes de Provence
- Salt and pepper to taste
- 8 whole-wheat lasagne sheets
- 200 g low-fat ricotta cheese
- 100 g grated mozzarella cheese (low GI, optional)
- Chopped fresh basil for garnish

INSTRUCTIONS

1. Preheat oven to 180°C (gas mark 6).
2. Heat the olive oil in a frying pan over medium heat. Add the chopped garlic and sauté until golden.
3. Add the slices of zucchini, eggplant and mushroom to the pan. Sauté for about 5 minutes, until slightly softened. Add the crushed tomatoes, tomato paste, herbes de Provence, salt and pepper. Simmer for 10 minutes.
4. Spread a thin layer of vegetable mixture in a gratin dish. Arrange a layer of lasagne sheets, then spread a layer of ricotta. Repeat until all ingredients are used up, finishing with a layer of vegetables.
5. If desired, sprinkle grated mozzarella cheese over the last layer of vegetables.
6. Cover with aluminum foil and bake for 30 minutes. Remove the foil and continue baking for a further 10 minutes, until the top is golden and the lasagne sheets are cooked.
7. Let stand a few minutes before serving. Garnish with chopped fresh basil before serving.

> Accompany this delicious vegetarian lasagne with a crisp green salad for acomplete and balanced meal.

WINTER VEGETABLE AND BARLEY FRITTERS

SERVINGS

Serves 4

PREPARATION TIME

15 minutes

COOKING TIME

40 minutes

INGREDIENTS

- 1 cup pearl barley
- 2 cups water
- 2 tablespoons olive oil
- 1 onion, chopped
- 2 carrots, diced
- 2 stalks celery, diced
- 200 g mushrooms, sliced
- 2 garlic cloves, minced
- 1 teaspoon dried thyme
- Salt and pepper to taste
- A few chopped fresh parsley leaves for garnish

INSTRUCTIONS

1. Rinse barley under cold water using a fine strainer. In a saucepan, bring 2 cups of water to a boil, then add the barley. Reduce heat, cover and simmer for 30 to 35 minutes, or until barley is tender. Drain and set aside.

2. In a large skillet, heat olive oil over medium heat. Add chopped onion and sauté for 2 – 3 minutes until translucent.

3. Add the diced carrots and celery to the pan. Sauté for 5 minutes until they begin to soften.

4. Add the sliced mushrooms and minced garlic to the pan. Sauté for 5 – 7 minutes until mushrooms are golden.

5. Add the cooked barley to the pan with the vegetables. Season with dried thyme, salt and pepper. Stir gently and simmer for 3 – 5 minutes.

6. Adjust seasoning if necessary. Serve hot, garnished with chopped fresh parsley.

> This pan-fried winter vegetables with barley can be served as is, or with a portion of vegetable protein such as grilled tofu for a balanced meal.

ZUCCHINI STUFFED WITH VEGETABLES AND QUINOA

SERVINGS

Serves 4

PREPARATION TIME

20 minutes

COOKING TIME

30 minutes

INGREDIENTS

- 4 medium-sized zucchini
- 1 cup cooked quinoa
- 1 tablespoon olive oil
- 1 onion, chopped
- 2 cloves garlic, minced
- 1 red bell pepper, diced
- Salt and pepper to taste
- 200 g mushrooms, sliced
- 400 g canned crushed tomatoes
- 1 teaspoon dried oregano
- 50 g crumbled goat's cheese (optional, low GI)
- Chopped fresh parsley for garnish

INSTRUCTIONS

1. Preheat oven to 180°C (gas mark 6).
2. Wash the zucchinis and cut them in half lengthways. Carefully scoop out the insides of the zucchinis with a spoon to form shells. Reserve the zucchini flesh.
3. Heat the olive oil in a frying pan over medium heat. Add the chopped onion and minced garlic. Sauté for 2 – 3 minutes until tender.
4. Add the red bell pepper, sliced mushrooms and zucchini flesh to the pan. Sauté for 5 minutes.
5. Stir in crushed tomatoes, cooked quinoa, dried oregano, salt and pepper. Mix well and simmer for 5 minutes.
6. Fill the hollowed-out zucchini halves with the vegetable and quinoa mixture. Arrange in an ovenproof dish.
7. If desired, sprinkle the crumbled goat's cheese over the top of the stuffed zucchinis.
8. Bake for 25 – 30 minutes, until the zucchinis are tender.
9. Garnish with chopped fresh parsley before serving.

> Serve these zucchini stuffed with vegetables and quinoa warm, with a green salad for a complete meal with a low glycemic index.

PEPPERS STUFFED WITH VEGETABLES AND BROWN RICE

SERVINGS

Serves 4

PREPARATION TIME

20 minutes

COOKING TIME

30 minutes

INGREDIENTS

- 4 large peppers (red, yellow or green)
- 1 cup cooked brown rice
- 1 tablespoon olive oil
- 1 onion, chopped
- 2 garlic cloves, minced
- 2 carrots, finely diced
- 1 zucchini, finely diced
- 200 g mushrooms, chopped
- 400 g canned crushed tomatoes
- 1 teaspoon herbes de Provence
- Salt and pepper to taste
- Grated cheese (optional, low GI)
- Chopped fresh parsley for garnish

INSTRUCTIONS

1. Preheat oven to 180°C (gas mark 6).
2. Wash the peppers, cut off the caps and remove the seeds and membranes. Set aside.
3. Heat the olive oil in a large frying pan over medium heat. Add the chopped onion and minced garlic. Sauté for 2 – 3 minutes until translucent.
4. Add the carrots, zucchini and mushrooms to the pan. Sauté for 5 minutes until they begin to soften.
5. Add the crushed tomatoes, herbes de Provence, salt and pepper. Simmer for 10 minutes over low heat.
6. Add the cooked rice to the vegetable mixture in the pan. Mix well.
7. Fill the hollowed-out peppers with the vegetable and rice mixture.
8. Arrange the stuffed peppers in an ovenproof dish. If desired, sprinkle grated cheese over the top of the stuffed peppers.
9. Bake for 25 – 30 minutes, until the peppers are tender.
10. Garnish with chopped fresh parsley before serving.

> Serve these peppers stuffed with vegetables and brown rice hot, accompanied by a green salad for a healthy, balanced meal with a low glycemic index.

SUMMER VEGETABLE TART

SERVINGS

Serves 4-6

PREPARATION TIME

20 minutes

COOKING TIME

30 – 35 minutes

INGREDIENTS

- ✔ 1 shortcrust or puff pastry
- ✔ 2 medium-sized zucchini
- ✔ 1 red bell pepper
- ✔ 1 yellow bell pepper
- ✔ 1 red onion
- ✔ 200 g cherry tomatoes
- ✔ 200 ml light crème fraîche
- ✔ 100 g grated cheese (optional, low GI)
- ✔ 2 tablespoons olive oil
- ✔ 3 eggs
- ✔ Salt and pepper to taste
- ✔ Fresh herbs (basil, oregano) for garnish

INSTRUCTIONS

1. Preheat oven to 180°C (gas mark 6).
2. Spread the pastry in a buttered tart tin and prick with a fork. Set aside in the fridge.
3. Wash and thinly slice all the vegetables.
4. Heat the olive oil in a frying pan over medium heat. Fry the onion until golden.
5. Arrange the slices of zucchini, bell pepper and cherry tomatoes on the pastry in the tart tin, alternating them nicely.
6. In a bowl, beat the eggs with the crème fraîche. Season with salt and pepper.
7. Pour this mixture over the vegetables in the tart tin. Make sure the liquid is evenly distributed.
8. If desired, sprinkle grated cheese over the top of the tart.
9. Bake for 30 – 35 minutes, or until golden brown and filling is set.
10. Let stand a few minutes before serving. Garnish with a few fresh herbs before serving.

> Serve this delicious summer vegetable tart warm or hot, with a green salad for a balanced meal rich in low-glycemic flavors.

TASTY DINNERS

Light, balanced dinners

SPINACH SALAD WITH STRAWBERRIES AND WALNUTS

SERVINGS

For 2 servings

PREPARATION TIME

15 minutes

INGREDIENTS

- 150 g fresh spinach
- 200 g fresh strawberries, sliced
- 1 ripe avocado, diced
- 30 g chopped walnuts
- 50 g fresh goat's cheese (optional, low GI)

Vinaigrette

- 2 tablespoons olive oil
- 1 tablespoon balsamic vinegar
- 1 teaspoon honey (optional, low GI)
- Salt and pepper to taste

INSTRUCTIONS

1. Wash the fresh spinach thoroughly and pat dry with a paper towel. Arrange in a large salad bowl.
2. Add the sliced strawberries and diced avocado to the spinach.
3. In a small frying pan over medium heat, lightly toast the crushed walnuts for a few minutes. Remove from the heat and leave to cool.
4. Add the toasted walnuts to the salad.
5. In a small bowl, prepare the vinaigrette by mixing the olive oil, balsamic vinegar, honey (if using), salt and pepper.
6. Pour the dressing over the salad and toss gently to coat all the ingredients.
7. If you're using goat's cheese, crumble it over the top of the salad.

> Serve Spinach Salad with Strawberries and Walnuts on individual plates. This salad can be accompanied by toast for a light, balanced, low-glycemic dinner.

PAN-FRIED SUMMER VEGETABLES WITH GRILLED TOFU

SERVINGS

For 2 servings

PREPARATION TIME

15 minutes

COOKING TIME

15 minutes

INGREDIENTS

- 200 g firm tofu
- 2 tablespoons olive oil
- 1 red bell pepper, cut into strips
- 1 zucchini, sliced into rings
- 1 red onion, thinly sliced
- 2 garlic cloves, chopped
- 150 g cherry tomatoes, halved
- 1 teaspoon dried oregano
- Salt and pepper to taste
- A few fresh basil leaves for garnish

INSTRUCTIONS

1. Drain and gently press the tofu to remove excess liquid. Cut into cubes.
2. Heat a tablespoon of olive oil in a frying pan over medium heat. Add the tofu cubes and brown them on each side for about 5 minutes. Remove from the pan and set aside.
3. In the same pan, add a tablespoon of olive oil. Sauté the minced onion and chopped garlic for 2 – 3 minutes, until translucent.
4. Add the bell pepper strips and zucchini slices to the pan. Sauté for 5 minutes.
5. Add the halved cherry tomatoes to the pan with the vegetables. Season with dried oregano, salt and pepper. Cook for 3 – 4 minutes, until the vegetables are tender but still crunchy.
6. Return the grilled tofu to the pan with the vegetables to warm up briefly.
7. Serve the pan-fried summer vegetables with grilled tofu on plates, garnished with fresh basil leaves.

> This pan-fried summer vegetables with grilled tofu is a light, balanced meal with a low glycemic index. Serve with cooked quinoa or brown rice for a complete meal.

VEGETABLE CURRY WITH COCONUT MILK

SERVINGS

Serves 4

PREPARATION TIME

15 minutes

COOKING TIME

25 minutes

INGREDIENTS

- 2 tablespoons coconut oil
- 1 onion, chopped
- 2 garlic cloves, minced
- 1 tablespoon curry paste
- 1 red bell pepper, cut into strips
- 2 carrots, sliced
- 1 eggplant, diced
- 400 ml coconut milk
- 1 cup cooked chickpeas
- Salt and pepper to taste
- Chopped fresh coriander for garnish (optional, low GI)

INSTRUCTIONS

1. Heat the coconut oil in a large frying pan over medium heat. Add the onion and garlic and sauté until golden and fragrant.
2. Add the curry paste to the pan and stir for a minute or so to release the aromas.
3. Add the red bell pepper, carrots and eggplant to the pan. Sauté vegetables for 5 minutes.
4. Pour the coconut milk into the pan and simmer over low heat for 15 – 20 minutes, until the vegetables are tender.
5. Add the chickpeas to the pan and simmer for a few more minutes to warm them up.
6. Season to taste with salt and pepper.
7. Remove from heat and let stand a few minutes before serving.
8. Just before serving, garnish each portion of vegetable curry with chopped fresh coriander, if desired.

> Arrange the coconut milk vegetable curry in bowls or soup plates. Serve with cooked quinoa or basmati rice for a complete and balanced meal with a low glycemic index.

RATATOUILLE WITH HERBS AND QUINOA

SERVINGS

Serves 4

PREPARATION TIME

15 minutes

COOKING TIME

30 minutes

INGREDIENTS

- ✔ 1 cup cooked quinoa
- ✔ 2 tablespoons olive oil
- ✔ 1 onion, chopped
- ✔ 2 garlic cloves, chopped
- ✔ 1 eggplant, diced
- ✔ 1 zucchini, diced
- ✔ 1 red bell pepper, diced
- ✔ 2 tomatoes, diced
- ✔ 2 tablespoons tomato paste
- ✔ 1 teaspoon dried herbes de Provence
- ✔ Salt and pepper to taste
- ✔ A few fresh basil leaves for garnish

INSTRUCTIONS

1. Cook quinoa according to package instructions and set aside.
2. Heat the olive oil in a large frying pan over medium heat. Add the chopped onion and sauté until translucent.
3. Add the chopped garlic and cook for a further minute.
4. Add the eggplant, zucchini and red bell pepper to the pan. Sauté for 8 – 10 minutes, until the vegetables begin to soften.
5. Stir in diced tomatoes, tomato paste and herbes de Provence. Season with salt and pepper. Simmer for 10 minutes over low heat.
6. Add the cooked quinoa to the ratatouille and toss gently to coat.
7. Garnish with fresh basil leaves before serving.

> Serve this ratatouille with herbs and quinoa warm, with a few slices of toasted wholemeal bread or a green salad for a light, balanced, low-glycemic dinner.

VEGETABLE AND CHICKPEA CURRY

SERVINGS

Serves 4

PREPARATION TIME

15 minutes

COOKING TIME

25 minutes

INGREDIENTS

- 1 can chickpeas, drained
- 2 tablespoons olive oil
- 1 onion, chopped
- 2 cloves garlic, minced
- 1 tablespoon curry paste
- 400 ml coconut milk
- 2 carrots, diced
- 1 zucchini, diced
- 1 red bell pepper, cut into strips
- Salt and pepper to taste
- A few fresh coriander leaves for garnish

INSTRUCTIONS

1. Heat the olive oil in a large frying pan over medium heat. Add the chopped onion and sauté until translucent.
2. Add the minced garlic and curry paste to the pan. Cook for 1 – 2 minutes to release the aromas.
3. Pour the coconut milk into the pan and mix well with the onions and curry paste.
4. Add the carrots, zucchini and bell pepper strips to the pan. Simmer for about 10 minutes, or until the vegetables are tender-crisp.
5. Add the drained chickpeas to the pan and heat for a few minutes.
6. Season to taste with salt and pepper.
7. Serve the vegetable and chickpea curry hot, garnished with fresh coriander leaves.

> Pair this vegetable and chickpea curry with a portion of basmati rice or quinoa for a tasty, low-glycemic dinner.

EXQUISITE DESSERTS

Sweet options with fresh and dried fruit

FRESH AND DRIED FRUIT SALAD WITH MINT

SERVINGS

Serves 4

PREPARATION TIME

15 minutes

INGREDIENTS

- 2 kiwis, peeled and diced
- 1 mango, peeled and diced
- 1 cup strawberries, chopped
- ½ cup raisins
- ½ cup pitted dates, chopped
- Juice of one lemon
- Fresh mint leaves for garnish
- 2 tablespoons maple syrup or honey (optional, low GI)

INSTRUCTIONS

1. In a large bowl, combine the diced kiwi, mango and strawberries.
2. Add the raisins and chopped dates to the fruit mixture.
3. Sprinkle lemon juice over the fruit to preserve its freshness and add a touch of tartness.
4. If you'd like a little extra sweetness, add 2 tablespoons of maple syrup or honey (optional).
5. Gently mix all the ingredients to coat the fruit with the juice.
6. Refrigerate the fruit salad for about 30 minutes to allow the flavors to mingle.

> Just before serving, garnish the fresh and dried fruit salad with fresh mint leaves for a touch of freshness. You can serve this salad in individual bowls or present it on a plate for a light, refreshing, low-glycemic dessert.

APPLE COMPOTE WITH DRIED FRUIT AND CINNAMON

SERVINGS

Serves 4

PREPARATION TIME

10 minutes

COOKING TIME

20 minutes

INGREDIENTS

- 4 apples, peeled, cored and diced
- ½ cup raisins
- ½ cup dried apricots, cut into pieces
- 2 tablespoons maple syrup or honey (optional, low GI)
- 1 teaspoon cinnamon powder
- ½ cup water
- Juice of one lemon
- Lemon zest for garnish (optional, low GI)

INSTRUCTIONS

1. In a saucepan, add the diced apples, raisins, dried apricot pieces, maple syrup or honey (if using), cinnamon, water and lemon juice.
2. Heat the mixture over medium-high heat until it begins to boil.
3. Reduce the heat and simmer for about 15 – 20 minutes, stirring occasionally, until the apples are tender and starting to break down.
4. Lightly mash the cooked apples with a spoon or fork to obtain a compote-like texture, leaving a few pieces for texture.
5. Remove from heat and allow to cool slightly.
6. Serve the dried-fruit applesauce warm or at room temperature. You can add lemon zest for a touch of freshness (optional).

> Serve the dried-fruit applesauce in individual bowls and garnish with lemon zest for a colorful presentation. This compote can also be enjoyed with a dollop of plain Greek yoghurt for a low-glycemic, high-protein dessert.

Exquisite desserts > Sweet options with fresh and dried fruit

WINTER FRUIT SALAD WITH WALNUTS

SERVINGS

Serves 4

PREPARATION TIME

15 minutes

INGREDIENTS

- ✔ 2 pears, peeled, seeded and diced
- ✔ 2 apples, peeled, cored and diced
- ✔ 1 orange, peeled and diced
- ✔ ½ cup walnut kernels, lightly toasted
- ✔ 2 tablespoons honey or maple syrup (optional, low GI)
- ✔ Juice of one lemon
- ✔ Lemon zest for garnish (optional, low GI)
- ✔ A few fresh mint leaves for garnish

INSTRUCTIONS

1. In a large bowl, combine the diced pears, apples and orange pieces.
2. Add the toasted walnuts to the fruit mixture.
3. Sprinkle lemon juice over the fruit to prevent oxidation and add a touch of acidity.
4. If desired, add 2 tablespoons of honey or maple syrup for extra sweetness.
5. Gently combine all ingredients to coat fruit with juice and sweetness.
6. Refrigerate the fruit salad for 15 to 20 minutes to allow the flavours to mingle.

Before serving, garnish the walnut winter fruit salad with lemon zest and a few fresh mint leaves for a refreshing presentation. Serve in individual bowls for a light, tasty, low-glycemic dessert.

SUMMER FRUIT CARPACCIO WITH ALMONDS

SERVINGS

Serves 4

PREPARATION TIME

15 minutes

INGREDIENTS

- 2 peaches, washed and thinly sliced
- 2 plums, washed and thinly sliced
- 1 cup strawberries, washed and thinly sliced
- ¼ cup slivered almonds, lightly toasted
- 2 tablespoons agave syrup or honey (optional, low GI)
- Juice of one lemon
- Lemon zest for garnish (optional, low GI)
- Fresh mint leaves for garnish

INSTRUCTIONS

1. Arrange peach, plum and strawberry slices artistically on individual plates or a large platter.
2. Sprinkle the toasted almonds over the fruit.
3. Lightly sprinkle the fruit with lemon juice for a tangy touch.
4. For extra sweetness, add 2 tablespoons of agave syrup or honey (optional).
5. Garnish with lemon zest and a few fresh mint leaves for a touch of freshness.

> Serve this almond summer fruit carpaccio beautifully arranged on individual plates. This presentation highlights the colorful beauty of the fruit and almonds. Perfect for a light, summery dessert with a low glycemic index.

GRILLED FRUIT SKEWERS WITH MINT

SERVINGS

Serves 4

PREPARATION TIME

15 minutes

COOKING TIME

5 – 7 minutes

INGREDIENTS

- 2 bananas, cut into thick slices
- 2 pears, quartered
- 2 kiwis, peeled and cut into pieces
- ½ cup strawberries, washed and hulled
- ½ cup pineapple, chopped
- ¼ cup honey or maple syrup (optional, low GI)
- Chopped fresh mint leaves for sprinkling

INSTRUCTIONS

1. Preheat your grill to medium heat.
2. Thread fruit pieces onto wooden or metal skewers in a variety of attractive ways.
3. If you're using honey or maple syrup, brush the skewers lightly with it for an extra sweet touch.
4. Place the skewers on the preheated grill and grill for approx. 2 – 3 minutes on each side, until the fruit is lightly caramelized.
5. Remove the skewers from the grill and sprinkle the grilled fruit with chopped fresh mint leaves.

> Present these delicious mint-roasted fruit skewers on a platter, accompanied by a mint yoghurt sauce or a scoop of vanilla ice cream for a refreshing low-glycemic dessert.

BOWL OF GREEK YOGURT WITH FRUIT AND NUTS

SERVINGS

Serves 4

PREPARATION TIME

10 minutes

INGREDIENTS

- ✔ 2 cups plain Greek yogurt
- ✔ 1 cup strawberries, washed and sliced
- ✔ 1 cup raspberries
- ✔ ½ cup blueberries
- ✔ ¼ cup crushed almonds, lightly toasted
- ✔ 2 tablespoons honey or maple syrup (optional, low GI)
- ✔ A few fresh mint leaves for garnish

INSTRUCTIONS

1. Divide the Greek yogurt between individual bowls.
2. Arrange the strawberry slices, raspberries and blueberries harmoniously over the yogurt.
3. Sprinkle with toasted almonds for added crunch.
4. If desired, lightly drizzle ½ tablespoon honey or maple syrup over each bowl for a light sweet aroma.
5. Garnish with fresh mint leaves for an extra touch of freshness.

Serve these bowls of fresh, lightly sweetened fruit and nut Greek yoghurt for a simple, satisfying low-glycemic dessert. They can be accompanied by a small oatmeal cookie or enjoyed as is for a natural sweetness.

LIGHT FRUIT MOUSSE

SERVINGS

Serves 4

PREPARATION TIME

15 minutes

INGREDIENTS

- ✔ 2 ripe bananas
- ✔ 1 ripe mango, peeled and diced
- ✔ 1 cup strawberries, washed and hulled
- ✔ Juice of one lemon
- ✔ ½ teaspoon vanilla (optional, low GI)
- ✔ 2 tablespoons plain Greek yogurt
- ✔ Fresh mint leaves for garnish

INSTRUCTIONS

1. In a blender, combine the bananas, mango and strawberries until smooth.
2. Add the lemon juice and vanilla (if using) to the fruit mixture and blend again to incorporate the flavors.
3. Gently fold the Greek yogurt into the fruit mixture for a smoother texture.
4. Divide the fruit mousse between individual bowls or verrines.
5. Chill in the refrigerator for at least 1 hour, until the mousse takes on a slightly firmer consistency.

> Before serving, garnish each cup with fresh mint leaves for a touch of freshness. This light, fragrant fruit mousse is perfect as a low-glycemic dessert, to be enjoyed on its own or with a few shortbread cookies for a crunchy touch.

EXOTIC FRUIT SALAD WITH COCONUT

SERVINGS

Serves 4

PREPARATION TIME

15 minutes

INGREDIENTS

- 1 ripe mango, peeled and diced
- 1 ripe papaya, peeled, seeded and diced
- 1 cup fresh pineapple, chopped
- ½ cup unsweetened shredded coconut
- Juice of one lime
- 2 tablespoons honey or maple syrup (optional, low GI)
- A few fresh mint leaves for garnish

INSTRUCTIONS

1. In a large bowl, combine the diced mango, papaya and pineapple chunks.
2. Add the shredded coconut to the fruit mixture.
3. Sprinkle the lime juice over the fruit for a tangy touch, and blend gently.
4. For a little extra sweetness, stir in 2 tablespoons honey or maple syrup (optional) and blend again.

> Serve this exotic coconut fruit salad in individual bowls and garnish with a few fresh mint leaves for a vibrant presentation. This salad is a delicious way to enjoy exotic fruits with a touch of coconut, while maintaining a low glycemic index for a refreshing dessert.

EXQUISITE DESSERTS

Light and balanced pastries

OATMEAL AND FRUIT MUFFINS

SERVINGS

For 12 muffins

PREPARATION TIME

15 minutes

COOKING TIME

20 – 25 minutes

INGREDIENTS

- 1½ cups oat flour
- ½ cup whole-wheat flour (moderate GI)
- 2 teaspoons baking powder
- ½ teaspoon baking soda
- ½ teaspoon salt
- 2 eggs
- ½ cup no-sugar-added applesauce
- ⅓ cup plain Greek yogurt
- ¼ cup melted coconut oil
- ¼ cup maple syrup or honey (optional, low GI)
- 1 teaspoon vanilla extract (optional, low GI)
- 1 cup chopped fresh fruit (strawberries, raspberries, blueberries)

INSTRUCTIONS

1. Preheat the oven to 180°C (350°F) and prepare a muffin tin with paper liners.
2. In a large bowl, combine the oat flour, whole-wheat flour, baking powder, baking soda and salt.
3. In another bowl, beat the eggs, then add the applesauce, Greek yogurt, melted coconut oil, maple syrup (or honey) and vanilla extract (if using). Mix well.
4. Add the liquid mixture to the dry ingredients and mix until combined. Do not overmix.
5. Gently fold the chopped fruit into the batter.
6. Divide the batter evenly between the muffin cases, filling them ¾ full.
7. Bake in a preheated oven for 20 – 25 minutes, or until a toothpick inserted in the center comes out clean.

> Let the muffins cool before serving. Arrange on a decorative plate and sprinkle lightly with additional oatmeal or fruit for an attractive presentation. These oat and fruit muffins are perfect for a light, balanced, low-glycemic dessert.

BANANA AND ALMOND COOKIES

SERVINGS

For 12 cookies

PREPARATION TIME

10 minutes

COOKING TIME

12 – 15 minutes

INGREDIENTS

- ✓ 2 ripe bananas, mashed
- ✓ 1½ cups rolled oats
- ✓ ½ cup crushed almonds
- ✓ ¼ cup high-cocoa dark chocolate chips (optional, low GI)
- ✓ 1 teaspoon cinnamon powder (optional, low GI)

INSTRUCTIONS

1. Preheat the oven to 180°C (350°F) and line a baking sheet with parchment paper.
2. In a bowl, combine the mashed bananas, rolled oats, chopped almonds, chocolate chips (if using) and cinnamon (if using). Mix well to form a smooth paste.
3. Using a tablespoon, scoop out portions of dough and place them on the baking sheet, spacing them to form cookies.
4. Using a slightly moistened fork, lightly flatten each cookie.
5. Bake for 12 – 15 minutes, until lightly browned.
6. Cool on a wire rack before serving.

> Arrange these delicious banana-almond cookies on a beautifully presented plate. These tasty, low-sugar cookies can be accompanied by a cup of tea or a glass of almond milk for a healthy, low-glycemic snack.

DATE AND WALNUT COOKIES

SERVINGS

For 12 cookies

PREPARATION TIME

15 minutes

COOKING TIME

12 – 15 minutes

INGREDIENTS

- 1 cup almond flour
- ½ cup rolled oats
- ½ teaspoon baking soda
- Pinch of salt
- ⅓ cup finely chopped dates
- ⅓ cup chopped nuts (almonds, hazelnuts or walnuts of your choice - low GI)
- 2 tablespoons melted coconut oil
- 1 tablespoon maple syrup or honey (optional, low GI)
- 1 teaspoon vanilla extract (optional, low GI)
- 1 egg

INSTRUCTIONS

1. Preheat the oven to 180°C (350°F) and line a baking sheet with parchment paper.
2. In a large bowl, combine the almond flour, rolled oats, baking soda and salt.
3. Add the chopped dates and chopped walnuts to the dry mixture and stir to incorporate.
4. In another bowl, beat the egg and add the melted coconut oil, maple syrup or honey (if using) and vanilla extract (if using). Mix well.
5. Add the liquid mixture to the dry ingredients and stir until smooth.
6. Shape the dough into tablespoon-sized balls and place them on the prepared baking sheet, spacing them slightly apart.
7. Flatten each ball slightly with the back of a spoon.
8. Bake for 12 – 15 minutes, or until lightly golden.
9. Cool on a wire rack before serving.

> Serve these date-nut cookies on a decorative plate. Pair with a cup of green tea or herbal tea for a low-glycemic treat.

COCONUT AND ALMOND ENERGY BITES

SERVINGS

For 12 bites

PREPARATION TIME

15 minutes

INGREDIENTS

- 1 cup unsweetened shredded coconut
- ½ cup almond flour
- ½ cup chopped almonds
- ⅓ cup maple syrup or honey
- 2 tablespoons melted coconut oil
- ½ teaspoon vanilla extract (optional, low GI)
- Pinch of salt

INSTRUCTIONS

1. In a large bowl, combine the shredded coconut, almond flour and chopped almonds.
2. Add the maple syrup or honey, melted coconut oil, vanilla extract (if using) and a pinch of salt. Mix well to form a dough.
3. Shape the dough into small balls and place on a plate.
4. Refrigerate for at least 30 minutes to harden slightly.

Arrange these coconut-almond energy bites on a plate. They're ready to enjoy as a light snack or healthy, low-glycemic dessert. You can also store them in an airtight container in the fridge for later use.

VANILLA AND ALMOND SHORTBREAD COOKIES

SERVINGS

For 12 cookies

PREPARATION TIME

20 minutes

COOKING TIME

12 – 15 minutes

INGREDIENTS

- ✔ 1 cup almond flour
- ✔ ¼ cup coconut flour
- ✔ ¼ cup melted coconut oil
- ✔ 3 tablespoons maple syrup or honey
- ✔ 1 teaspoon vanilla extract
- ✔ ¼ cup slivered almonds for garnish (optional)
- ✔ Pinch of salt

INSTRUCTIONS

1. Preheat the oven to 180°C (350°F) and line a baking sheet with parchment paper.
2. Mix the almond flour, coconut flour and a pinch of salt in a bowl.
3. Add the melted coconut oil, maple syrup or honey and vanilla extract to the flour mixture. Mix until smooth.
4. Shape the dough into tablespoon-sized balls and place them on the prepared baking sheet, spacing them slightly apart. Flatten slightly with the back of a spoon.
5. Garnish each cookie with flaked almonds (optional).
6. Bake for 12 – 15 minutes, or until lightly golden around the edges.
7. Cool on a wire rack before serving.

Arrange these vanilla-almond shortbread cookies on a beautifully presented plate. Serve with a cup of vanilla tea for a low-glycemic moment of indulgence.

COCONUT BITES WITH DRIED FRUIT

SERVINGS

For 12 bites

PREPARATION TIME

15 minutes

INGREDIENTS

- 1 cup unsweetened shredded coconut
- ¼ cup chia seeds
- ¼ cup finely chopped dates
- ¼ cup chopped nuts (almonds, hazelnuts, walnuts - low GI)
- 2 tablespoons maple syrup or honey
- 1 teaspoon vanilla extract
- Pinch of salt

INSTRUCTIONS

1. In a bowl, combine the shredded coconut, chia seeds, chopped dates and chopped walnuts.
2. Add the maple syrup or honey, vanilla extract and a pinch of salt. Mix well to form a sticky dough.
3. Shape the dough into small balls and place on a plate.
4. Refrigerate for at least 30 minutes to harden slightly.

Arrange these dried-fruit coconut bites on a plate. They're perfect as a light dessert or a healthy, low-glycemic snack. They can be stored in an airtight container in the fridge for later consumption.

BANANA AND DARK CHOCOLATE COOKIES

SERVINGS

For 12 cookies

PREPARATION TIME

15 minutes

COOKING TIME

12 – 15 minutes

INGREDIENTS

- ✔ 2 ripe bananas, mashed
- ✔ 1½ cups rolled oats
- ✔ ½ cup high-cocoa dark chocolate chips
- ✔ ¼ cup chopped nuts of your choice (almonds, cashews)
- ✔ 1 teaspoon vanilla extract
- ✔ Pinch of salt

INSTRUCTIONS

1. Preheat the oven to 180°C (350°F) and line a baking sheet with parchment paper.
2. In a large bowl, mix together the rolled oats, dark chocolate chips, chopped walnuts and a pinch of salt.
3. Add the mashed bananas and vanilla extract to the dry mixture. Mix well to obtain a homogeneous paste.
4. Spoon mounds of dough onto the prepared baking sheet, spacing them slightly apart. Flatten slightly with the back of a spoon.
5. Bake for 12 to 15 minutes, or until lightly golden around the edges.
6. Cool on a wire rack before serving.

Arrange these dark chocolate banana cookies on a plate. Serve with a cup of tea or a glass of almond milk for a tasty, low-glycemic snack.

EXQUISITE DESSERTS

Healthy alternatives to satisfy sweet cravings

COCONUT AND DRIED FRUIT ENERGY BALLS

SERVINGS

For 12 balls

PREPARATION TIME

15 minutes

INGREDIENTS

- 1 cup pitted dates
- ½ cup almonds
- ½ cup cashews
- ¼ cup unsweetened shredded coconut
- 2 tablespoons chia seeds
- 2 tablespoons melted coconut oil
- 1 teaspoon vanilla extract
- Pinch of salt

INSTRUCTIONS

1. In a food processor, combine dates, almonds, cashews, shredded coconut, chia seeds, melted coconut oil, vanilla extract and a pinch of salt. Blend to a sticky paste.
2. Scoop out portions of dough and roll them between your hands to form bite-sized balls.
3. Place the energy balls on a plate.
4. Refrigerate for at least 30 minutes to firm up.

Arrange the energy balls on a decorative plate. They're ready to enjoy as a light dessert or healthy, low-glycemic snack. Store in an airtight container in the fridge for later consumption.

RED FRUIT AND ALMOND CREAM TARTLETS

SERVINGS

For 6 tarts

PREPARATION TIME

20 minutes

COOKING TIME

15 – 20 minutes

INGREDIENTS

For the dough

- 1 cup almond flour
- 2 tablespoons melted coconut oil
- 1 tablespoon maple syrup (low GI, optional)
- Pinch of salt

For the almond cream

- ½ cup almond powder
- 2 tablespoons maple syrup (low GI, optional)
- 2 tablespoons almond milk
- 1 teaspoon almond extract
- 1 tablespoon cornstarch

For the trim

- Fresh red fruit (strawberries, raspberries, blueberries - low GI)

INSTRUCTIONS

1. Preheat oven to 180°C (350°F).
2. In a bowl, mix the almond flour, melted coconut oil, maple syrup (if using) and a pinch of salt to form a dough. Divide the dough into 6 equal portions.
3. Using your fingers, press each portion of dough into the bottom and up the sides of pre-greased tartlet molds. Prick the bottom with a fork.
4. Bake the tart shells for 10 – 12 minutes, until lightly browned.
5. Meanwhile, prepare the almond cream. In a bowl, mix the almond powder, maple syrup (if using), almond milk, almond extract and cornstarch until smooth.
6. Spread the cooled almond cream over the tart shells.
7. Arrange the fresh berries on top of the almond cream.
8. Refrigerate the tartlets for at least 1 hour before serving.

> Serve these red fruit and almond cream tartlets on individual plates. They're perfect as a light dessert to round off a meal, or for a low-glycemic gourmet break.

SUMMER FRUIT CHIA PUDDING

SERVINGS

Serves 4

PREPARATION TIME

10 minutes (+ temps de repos)

INGREDIENTS

- ½ cup chia seeds
- 2 cups unsweetened almond milk
- 2 tablespoons maple syrup or honey (low GI, optional)
- 1 teaspoon vanilla extract
- 2 cups summer fruit (strawberries, peaches, apricots) diced
- A few fresh mint leaves for garnish (optional)

INSTRUCTIONS

1. In a large bowl, combine chia seeds, almond milk, maple syrup or honey (if using) and vanilla extract. Stir well to combine all ingredients. Let stand for 10 minutes.
2. After 10 minutes, stir the mixture again to prevent the chia seeds from forming lumps. Cover the bowl and place in the fridge for at least 4 hours, or ideally overnight, to allow the pudding to thicken.
3. Just before serving, divide the chia pudding between verrines or bowls.
4. Add the diced summer fruit on top of the pudding.
5. Garnish with a few fresh mint leaves for an extra touch of freshness.

Present these summer fruit chia puddings in individual verrines or decorative bowls. They're perfect for a refreshing and healthy low-glycemic dessert, showcasing the freshness of seasonal fruit.

GREEK YOGURT WITH RED FRUIT AND ALMONDS

SERVINGS

Serves 4

PREPARATION TIME

10 minutes

INGREDIENTS

- ✔ 2 cups plain Greek yogurt
- ✔ 1 cup mixed berries (strawberries, raspberries, blueberries)
- ✔ ¼ cup slivered almonds
- ✔ 2 tablespoons honey or maple syrup (low GI, optional)
- ✔ A few fresh mint leaves for garnish (optional)

INSTRUCTIONS

1. Divide the Greek yogurt between four individual bowls.
2. Arrange the mixed berries over the yoghurt.
3. Lightly toast the slivered almonds in a dry frying pan until golden, then sprinkle over the red fruit.
4. If desired, add a tablespoon of honey or maple syrup for an extra touch of sweetness.
5. Garnish with a few fresh mint leaves for a touch of freshness.

Serve these bowls of Greek yoghurt with red fruits and almonds individually. It's a simple, refreshing, low-glycemic dessert, perfect for a light, healthy end to a meal.

CINNAMON APPLESAUCE

SERVINGS

Serves 4

PREPARATION TIME

10 minutes

COOKING TIME

15 minutes

INGREDIENTS

- 4 apples, peeled, cored and diced
- 1 tablespoon lemon juice
- 2 tablespoons water
- 1 teaspoon cinnamon powder
- 1 tablespoon honey or maple syrup (low GI, optional)
- Plain Greek yogurt (optional, to serve)

INSTRUCTIONS

1. In a saucepan over medium heat, combine the diced apples, lemon juice, water and cinnamon powder.
2. Simmer for about 10 to 15 minutes, stirring occasionally, until the apples are tender and starting to fall apart.
3. Lightly mash the cooked apples with a wooden spoon to obtain a more or less smooth compote consistency, according to your preference.
4. Add a tablespoon of honey or maple syrup to sweeten slightly, to taste.
5. Remove from heat and allow to cool slightly.
6. Serve the cinnamon applesauce warm or cold. You can also serve it with a dollop of plain Greek yoghurt for a delicious variation.

> Serve this cinnamon applesauce in individual bowls or verrines. It's a comforting dessert with a low glycemic index, perfect for a smooth end to a meal.

EXQUISITE DESSERTS

Frozen and gourmet desserts

RED FRUIT AND GREEK YOGURT POPSICLES

SERVINGS

For 6 popsicles

PREPARATION TIME

10 minutes (+ freezing time)

INGREDIENTS

- 1 cup plain Greek yogurt
- 1 cup mixed berries (strawberries, raspberries, blueberries)
- 2 tablespoons maple syrup or honey (low GI, optional)
- ½ teaspoon vanilla extract
- ¼ cup granola (optional, low GI)

INSTRUCTIONS

1. In a blender, combine the Greek yogurt, red berries, maple syrup or honey (if using) and vanilla extract. Blend until smooth.
2. If desired, add granola to the mixture for a crunchy texture.
3. Pour mixture into popsicle molds up to the top.
4. Insert popsicle sticks and freeze for at least 4 hours, or overnight.
5. To unmold, run the molds briefly under hot water to release the popsicles.

> Serve the red berry and Greek yoghurt popsicles on a platter or individual plate. For a more festive presentation, sprinkle some granola on top or add a few fresh red fruits for a colorful touch. It's a refreshing and delicious low-glycemic option to round off a meal, or for a frosty treat.

TROPICAL MANGO AND COCONUT SORBET

SERVINGS

Serves 4

PREPARATION TIME

10 minutes (+ freezing time)

INGREDIENTS

- 2 ripe mangoes, peeled and diced
- ½ cup coconut milk
- Juice of one lime
- 2 tablespoons agave syrup or honey (low GI, optional)
- ¼ cup unsweetened shredded coconut (low GI, optional)

INSTRUCTIONS

1. Place the diced mango in a blender with the coconut milk, lime juice and agave syrup or honey (if using).
2. Blend until smooth.
3. Pour the mixture into a shallow freezer dish.
4. Place the dish in the freezer and leave to set for around 1-2 hours.
5. Every 30 minutes, remove the dish from the freezer and gently scrape the top of the sorbet with a fork to break up any ice crystals. Repeat this step every 30 minutes until the sorbet is set and has an ice-cream texture.
6. To serve, scoop the sorbet into balls using an ice-cream scoop, and garnish with grated coconut if desired.

> Serve tropical mango and coconut sorbet in individual cups or bowls. Add a finishing touch by sprinkling shredded coconut on top for a refreshing summer presentation.

WATERMELON GRANITA

SERVINGS

Serves 4

PREPARATION TIME

10 minutes (+ freezing time)

INGREDIENTS

- 4 cups diced seedless watermelon
- Juice of half a lemon
- 2 tablespoons agave syrup or honey (low GI, optional)
- Fresh mint leaves for garnish (optional)

INSTRUCTIONS

1. Place the watermelon cubes in a blender with the lemon juice and agave syrup or honey (if using).
2. Blend until smooth.
3. Pour the watermelon purée into a shallow freezer dish.
4. Place the dish in the freezer and leave to freeze for around 2 hours.
5. Every 30 minutes, remove the dish from the freezer and scrape the surface of the granita with a fork to form ice crystals. Repeat until all the mixture has formed crystals.
6. To serve, divide the granita between individual glasses. Garnish with mint leaves for a touch of freshness.

Serve the watermelon granita in clear glasses to highlight its crystalline texture. Add a few fresh mint leaves for a fragrant, decorative touch.

FROZEN YOGURT AND BERRY STICKS

SERVINGS

For 6 sticks

PREPARATION TIME

10 minutes (+ freezing time)

INGREDIENTS

- 1 cup plain Greek yoghurt
- 1 cup mixed berries (strawberries, raspberries, blueberries - low GI)
- 2 tablespoons maple syrup or honey (low GI, optional)
- ½ teaspoon vanilla extract
- A few whole berries (for garnish, optional)

INSTRUCTIONS

1. In a blender, combine the Greek yogurt, mixed berries, maple syrup or honey (if using) and vanilla extract. Blend until smooth and homogeneous.
2. Pour mixture into popsicle molds up to the top.
3. Insert popsicle sticks and freeze for at least 4 hours, or overnight.
4. To unmold, briefly run the molds under hot water to release the popsicle sticks.
5. If desired, garnish each stick with a few whole berries before freezing.

> Present yogurt-berry popsicle sticks on a colorful tray or in individual popsicle holders. They're a refreshing, low-glycemic option for a healthy, gourmet dessert.

LEMONGRASS AND MINT GRANITA

SERVINGS

Serves 4

PREPARATION TIME

10 minutes (+ freezing time)

INGREDIENTS

- 4 cups water
- 4 lemongrass stalks, chopped
- ½ cup coconut sugar or agave syrup
- Juice of 2 lemons
- Fresh mint leaves for garnish (optional)

INSTRUCTIONS

1. In a saucepan, bring the water to the boil. Add the lemongrass and simmer for 5 minutes. Remove from the heat and leave to infuse for 10 – 15 minutes. Strain to remove any pieces of lemongrass.
2. Add coconut sugar or agave syrup to the still-hot lemongrass infusion. Stir to dissolve sugar completely. Leave to cool to room temperature.
3. Add the lemon juice to the cooled mixture and stir well.
4. Pour the mixture into a shallow freezer dish.
5. Place the dish in the freezer for at least 2 hours. Every 30 minutes, gently scrape the granita with a fork to form ice crystals.
6. To serve, divide the granita between individual bowls. Garnish with fresh mint leaves for a touch of freshness.

> Serve lemongrass and mint granita in dessert cups or bowls. Add fresh mint leaves for a refreshing presentation and a pleasant taste experience.

APPENDICES

Measurements and ingredients

Table of Glycemic Indexes for common foods

Here is a table showing some common foods and their approximate glycemic index (GI):

Food	Glycemic Index (GI)
Oats (unprocessed)	55
Basmati rice	58-63
Quinoa	53
Potatoes	70-80
Sweet potatoes	44-77
Wholemeal bread	50-70
Pulses (lentils, peas)	25-45
Banana	42-62
Apple	36-52
Pear	38-53
Nuts (almonds, walnuts)	Low
Plain Greek yogurt	11
Cooked carrots	39
Chickpeas	28-42
Black beans	30
Lentils	30-52
Dark chocolate (70% cocoa)	23-50
Orange juice	50
Sweet potato	44-77

Note: Glycemic index values may vary depending on a number of factors, such as food preparation, ripeness and combination with other foods in a meal. Use these values as a general reference to guide your food choices towards low-GI consumption.

Appendices > **Measurements and ingredients** | 243

Conversion of measures to facilitate book use

To make the book easier to use, here is a conversion table for measurements commonly used in recipes:

Measures	Conversion
Grams (g)	1 gram = 0.0353 ounces
Ounces (oz)	1 ounce = 28.35 grams
Milliliters (ml)	1 milliliter = 0.0338 ounces
Liters (l)	1 liter = 33.814 ounces
Coffee spoon	1 teaspoon = 5 ml
Soup spoon	1 tablespoon = 15 ml
Cup	1 cup = 236.6 millilitres

List of essential low-GI vegetarian ingredients to have in your kitchen

A list of low-glycemic vegetarian ingredients that are essential to have in your kitchen for concocting healthy, balanced meals:

Pulses

- Lentils (green, coral)
- Black beans
- Chickpeas
- Kidney beans
- Tofu or tempeh

Wholegrain cereals

- Quinoa
- Whole grain rice
- Buckwheat
- Barley
- Spelt or wholemeal flour

244 | Appendices > Measurements and ingredients

Fresh and frozen vegetables

- Spinach
- Broccoli
- Peppers
- Zucchinis
- Tomatoes

Fresh and dried fruit

- Apples
- Pears
- Plums
- Berries (raspberries, strawberries, blueberries)
- Raisins or dates

Plant-based dairy products

- Unsweetened almond milk
- Unsweetened soy milk
- Plain soy yogurt

Nuts and seeds

- Almonds
- Cashew nuts
- Chia seeds
- Flax seeds
- Walnuts

Natural sweeteners

- Maple syrup or agave syrup
- Natural Stevia
- Coconut sugar

Healthy oils and fats

- Extra virgin olive oil
- Coconut oil
- Avocados

Spices and herbs

- Turmeric
- Cinnamon
- Paprika
- Parsley
- Basil

> These ingredients form a solid basis for preparing low-glycemic meals for vegetarians. Having them on hand makes it easier to cook a variety of dishes, rich in nutrients and flavors, while maintaining optimal glycemic balance. This list offers a variety of options for creating tasty, nourishing recipes as part of a vegetarian diet geared to a low glycemic index.

From the same author

Did you like this book?

You can leave a review on its page

Printed in Great Britain
by Amazon